Neighs and Whispers

A study of contact and communication with horses

First published by Nottingham University Press

This reissued original edition published 2023 by 5m Books Ltd www.5mbooks.com

Neighs and Whispers: A study of contact and communication with horses
Original title: RELINCHOS Y SUSURROS. Un estudio acerca del contacto y la comunicación con los caballos.

Publisher: Editorial Maipue in arrangement with
Nottingham University Press
University of Nottingham
King's Meadow Campus
Lenton Lane
Nottingham NG7 2NR

Translation: Bárbara Strugatz and Cecilia Martínez

E-mail: ventas@maipue.com.ar / promocion@maipue.com.ar
www.maipue.com.ar

All rights reserved. No part of this publication may be reproduced in any material form (including photocopying or storing in any medium by electronic means and whether or not transiently or incidentally to some other use of this publication) without the written permission of the copyright holder except in accordance with the provisions of the Copyright, Designs and Patents Act 1988. Applications for the copyright holder's written permission to reproduce any part of this publication should be addressed to the publishers.

British Library Cataloguing in Publication Data

Neighs and Whispers: A study of contact and communication with horses
A Zlotnik

ISBN 9781789182934

English translation first published 2012
Copyright © Editorial Maipue 2012

Inside photographs: Adriana Boess, Anahí Zlotnik, Constantino Sánchez Martínez, Danae Van Bortel, Gonzalo Cantero, Marcelo Zazzeri

Typeset by Nottingham University Press, Nottingham
EU GPSR Authorised Representative
LOGOS EUROPE, 9 rue Nicolas Poussin, 17000, LA ROCHELLE, France
E-mail: Contact@logoseurope.eu

Neighs and Whispers

A study of contact and communication with horses

Anahí Zlotnik

CONTENTS

PROLOGUE	xi
DEDICATION	xiii
ACKNOWLEDGEMENTS	xv
INTRODUCTION	xvii
TAKHI, THE WILD HORSE	**1**
Equus Main Features	6
Physical characteristics	6
Mental characteristics	7
Where do horses stand in the animal scale?	8
Class Mammals (Mammalia)	8
Order Ungulates (Ungulata)	8
Perissodactyl Suborder (Perissodactyla)	8
HOW DO HORSES COMMUNICATE?	**9**
How Does Vocal Communication Work?	15
Horses whisper	16
They also squeal	17
They sometimes snort or puff	17
They roar when they are angry	18
How Do They Express Themselves Through Their Body?	18
Warning or "something new is happening to me" posture	19
How do they express themselves with their tail?	19
My horse's ears swing to and fro	20
The mouth is not just for eating	21
What is the Flehmen response?	22

What are pheromones?	23
How do they express themselves through their nostrils?	24
They express so much with their head!	25
Soft contact	25
The neck is beautiful	26
This horse is a dancer!	26
The croup	27
Hooves and legs	27
How do they threaten?	28
How do other horses respond to threats?	29

HORSES HAVE BRAINS AND FEELINGS — 31

Why This Title?	33
Vegetative Potential	34
Sensory Potential	34
Cognitive activity	34
Appetising activity	37
What Is The Horse's Nervous System Like?	39
How Does Memory Work?	45

LEARNING — 49

What Does Learning Mean For A Social Animal?	51
What Is A Genetic Program?	52
What Is Training?	53
Different Ways Of Learning	53
Non-associative learning or habituation	54
Learning by conditioning or association	55
Imprinting or engraving	58
Learning through observation or social learning (imitative or by emulation)	62
Silent or exploratory learning (latent)	63

Discernment (insight) or problem solving	64
Different types of learning	65

TEACHING AND GAMES — 67

- Gnomo — 69
- Teaching – Training — 71
  - What is the aim of teaching? — 73
  - When do handling problems appear? — 73
  - What happens with punishment? — 74
  - Horses are a perfect mirror of the riders — 75
  - Negative habits — 76
  - Obedience — 77
  - The best reward — 78
  - Animal's condition — 79
  - Attention factor — 79
  - How do we avoid tension? — 80
  - Responsible trainers — 81
  - Spontaneous answers — 81
  - What does observing the steps mean? — 82
  - The useful effort — 83
  - Intuition — 84
  - When is punishment effective? — 84
  - Gestalt thinking — 84
  - Why do many people get angry with their horses? — 85
  - What is passive leadership? — 86
- Some Aspects Of The Work With Foals — 89
  - What is early stimulation? — 89
  - Familiarisation — 90
  - Games stimulate intelligence — 92
  - Game functions — 92
  - The case of a filly who did not socialise — 93

INTELLIGENCE AND LEADERSHIP — 95
What Is Intelligence? — 97
- Why do we talk about the intelligence of horses? — 98
- Their nature — 98
- Their characteristics and abilities - According to Robert Miller DVM — 99
- Hierarchy and submission – Biological function — 100

Leadership — 101
- What are the advantages of the hierarchical system? — 103
- What is the function of dominance? — 104
- What is the function of submission? — 104
- Do horses make decisions? — 105
- How do they use stimuli? — 105
- Do they feel frustration? — 105
- Stimuli and responses — 106
- Evolution and adaptation — 107
- Campero — 109

COMMUNICATION — 113
Malenki And Jadrift. Unusual Communication Phenomena — 117
- Morphic Fields — 120
- Synchrony — 123
- Intention — 124
- Different cognitive states — 125
- Personality and identity — 126

WHAT CAN WE LEARN FROM THE MOST INTELLIGENT HORSES? — 129
Case I - Monte, A Racing Horse — 129
Case II - A Terrified Little Horse — 137
- Working Technique — 143
- First Step: Diagnosis — 143

Second step: Develop a prognosis … 143
Third Step: Medication … 144
Fourth Step: Change of circumstances … 145
Fifth step: Desensitisation … 146
Sixth (and last) step: Memory – Leaving him with the best memory … 146
Conclusion … 146

Case III - PURITA … 149
A Mare From Whom I Learnt A Lot … 151
Treatment Aims … 152
The man, the snake and the stone … 156

PROLOGUE

Heads of four horses (Oskar Merte, 19th – 20th c.)

> *"We have caused life a huge damage by taking away its mystery"*
>
> R.M. RILKE

The horse is an animal that has accompanied man since the earliest times. For him, the horse has always symbolised different qualities either in his daily life, at work, leisure, in dreams and in the spiritual world. We should remember that horses are present in numerous holy books of Central Asia and the Far East.

Goodness of heart and dignity, strength and spirit, speed and balance, are some of the qualities that may arise when one observes a wild colt.

This simple but profound book represents a bridge towards that mystery of strength and intelligence that is the horse. It is a valuable contribution to the serious study of animal behaviour and an excellent metaphor in which the horse represents instinct and intuition, while the author represents the eye of science that is, in this case, subtle, tender and kind.

GABRIEL FIGINI

DEDICATION

This book is dedicated to all those people who love horses and enjoy being with them, either jumping, running, taking part in any equestrian activity, or simply through the pure pleasure of riding them and taking care of them.

I want to specially dedicate this book to my instructor, my parents and friends, who insisted for a long time that I rebuild the bond with horses, and particularly to my friends: Gnomo, Brisel, Malenki, Ancar, Negrito, Jadrift, and their foal Nasruddina and Frutillito, Purita, Sevillana, Jazmín, Alicia, Malvina, Haram, Antonio, Kilbracken, Rosato, Mustang, Gran Bet, Martina Girl, La Voluntad and Monte Embarcado.

I also dedicate it to the men and horses for rent from Rio Tercero, Cordoba, who taught me about their everyday life and who gave me my first horse, which I could not bring to Buenos Aires. A blond, light-eyed, overo young mare who fell asleep when I stroked her, and whom the men from the rental named Anahí.

And to all the horses I met since I was a child: the horse of the man who delivered water, the baker's horse and the greengrocer's, who walked by my front door; to the horse of the man who sold wicker, who covered his neck to prevent him from getting sunstroke; to the ones who attended my courses; and to all my patients, who bring so much joy to my heart.

Because they made me dream of a world of ladies and gentlemen, where word, honor and justice were real values. Because I could play with them and make a circus in the street where I lived, in my hometown. A circus with a white cart horse, over which I danced with my butterfly costume, on the street with my friends, who played at being laborers. Because I still long for a place where horses can live without being hurt. Because of the passion and the willingness to know and understand them that they aroused in me, because of their generosity, and because they helped me during the saddest moments of my childhood.

Because they woke up in me a feeling of unity and protection, for which I am truly grateful. Thanks to them, I studied Veterinary Science, and thanks to them I travel to different places to teach my courses.

And because I have always felt attracted to their look, a deep, warm look. A mystery made of wind and fire. My friend, the horse.

ACKNOWLEDGMENTS

To those persons who helped, encouraged me and were there for me and continue encouraging me in this research of communication with horses.

To my parents, who made a great effort so I could be near horses and have horses.

To my instructor, Agha, for guiding me with love and patience.

To Gabriel Figini, for supporting my ideas, hopes and dreams and for helping me to materialise them.

To Diana Maclean, for sharing her passion for horses and for the rich exchange of experiences.

To María Dolores Murtagh, my assistant for two years, who contributed with productive ideas and who was very good company.

To Adriana Boess for her constant enthusiasm, her creative ideas, company and pictures.

To my colleague, Juan. C. Martín, for sharing his experience with me and for letting me prove that this work method positively influences horses' lives.

To Robert M. Miller D.V.M, from the United States, for allowing me to translate his article.

To the organisers and participants of the courses in Argentina and Spain, and to those who provide their places and horses to that end.

Anahí Zlotnik

INTRODUCTION: HORSE BEHAVIOUR

Running away (Gauguin – 1901)

Horses have always been and are my soul mates even before I uttered my first words. According to my mother, when I was a little girl the first time I ever saw a horse my face was filled with joy; in fact I have not lost that feeling, when I am with them, mounting, watching or treating them as a veterinarian.

Their subtle world, expressed by means of their silent body language, has always drawn my attention because it is a way of getting to know them and to know myself. So I have been studying their behavior and their way of communicating among themselves and between us and them.

I cannot be but surprised as to their qualities and different ways of reacting and communicating. I find their world mysterious and very vast, and it keeps inviting me to investigate them with dedication and patience.

This book is the result of my experience as a veterinarian, trainer and horsewoman and from the study of a reliable and verified bibliography. It does not claim to be a

> *Ethology: (gr. èthos, habits, and logos, discourse). Scientific study of animal behavior.*

behaviour guide or an instruction manual. As a veterinarian, my intention is to transmit my experience in the use of behavioural therapy with my patients who, in general, are stabled animals or live free within small paddock or bigger pastures. Some of these horses are under great stress, tension, ill-treatment or bad handling and, as a result, they have developed behaviour disorders.

I believe that every study carried out with wild horses, feral horses (animals who have escaped from reservations or farmhouses and live in a wild state) or that have been carried out in universities or other places where one can observe their behavior under certain conditions and circumstances, is useful because they provide information about this particular species. This is absolutely necessary to be able to understand horses, and it can be used in different situations throughout their entire life.

In this book, you will find information regarding the way they communicate, about their social life under certain circumstances and how we can understand what is happening to them. There are also anecdotes, stories about horses I have met or stories that my students, colleagues or friends have told me, experiences with ill-treated horses, the rehabilitation work, how to read their signs without misinterpreting them, and some basic techniques to begin a different relationship with our quadruped friends. This information is provided with cases I have experienced. It is important to comprehend horse reactions during massages, when we ride them, when we teach them or when they need retraining in case of behaviour disorders.

The aim is to approach the horse with an open, flexible and subtle look in order to understand their world and improve their quality of life.

In the 20th century the Austrian zoologist and philosopher, Konrad Lorenz, told through his books different experiences with geese, dogs and birds. In those books he described the varied behaviors of those animals - this type of study is called ethology.

Nowadays, "old" techniques are being recognised once again in relationship to horse education, training, unconventional preventive and curative medicine that some people call "alternative". Why? Because man needs to observe nature again, get to know its laws, the behaviour of each species in order to understand horses and to understand themselves.

Interaction with other species that live on our planet encourages a balance and harmony of life in this world. It is part of an evolutionary process that is occurring across the whole planet: more and better communication, different ways of communication, better education, more information and receptiveness to new sciences such as ethology, psychology, biology and physics.

The horse, just like other domestic species, has descended from its wild ancestors and in its way through evolution, adaptation and natural selection, has had to develop diverse strategies in order to survive. One of these survival strategies, both in the wild and domestic states, is flight at great speed in a short time to escape from predators such as the huge felines and wolves that are quite shrewd, fast and quick. In this way, the horse evolved and adapted transforming itself into a fast, short distance sprinter. From an anatomical, physiological and ethological perspective, it is perfectly adapted for that function.

Being the target of predators forced it to develop perception to a degree of subtlety that is difficult to perceive by the average man. According to Dr. Robert M. Miller, American veterinarian and specialist in equine ethology, the horse is the most perceptive of domestic animals.

Because of this quality, many people misinterpret their reactions or get confused. Horses possess acute and bright external senses, a capacity that allows them to perceive certain environmental situations that the average man is incapable of detecting; horses anticipate those situations and react to them because they are a prey species. Those people who believe horses are dumb or aggressive because they react in a certain way, are incapable of understanding that horses react to something that, for men, being predators, is not dangerous, but could be for horses.

In order to illustrate this lack of comprehension, this tale from Eastern tradition might be helpful:

An idiot looked at a browsing camel. He said to it:

'Your appearance is awry. Why is this so?'

The camel replied: 'In judging the impression made, you are attributing a fault to that which shaped the form. Be aware of this! Do not consider my crooked appearance a fault. 'Get away from me, by the shortest route. My appearance is thus for function, for a reason. The bow needs the bentness as well as the straightness of the bowstring. 'Fool, begone! An ass's perception goes with an ass's nature.'

For being smart, with a good memory and sensitive, horses can be easily desensitised under negative stimuli such as fear, punishment and stress and, for the same reason, you can condition them or create positive reinforcements to positive and pleasant stimuli. By means of behaviour therapy, a negative behavior can be replaced with a positive one, something that must be done in a gentle way, patiently and intelligently. In a way, this is what Indians, Bedouins, or Middle East tribes did. They had a close contact with their horses due to their need for survival.

They raised them, observed them and had a profound knowledge of them; they lived together day and night so that, in a certain way, they could transform themselves into horses so as to make contact with them. It is said that *in order to know the stone, you have to transform yourself into a stone*. When you get to know something, you become that something. In reference to Saint Francis of Assisi who claimed that animals were our little brothers, for them, the horse was like a little brother.

The aim of this way of working is to improve the man-horse relationship, making it an agreeable relationship for both parts. If we learn to understand their way of communication – their silent body language, their signs, habits and behavior – we will acquire more and better instruments to educate them so as to optimally develop their full potential.

What is desensitisation? It is a process by which we replace a negative behavior with a positive one. Horses are easily desensitised. Why? Because if they were not accustomed to certain harmless stimuli in their natural life, they would feel obliged to sprint the whole time. So horses are naturally prepared to decide whether a stimulus is a real danger or not, as in the case of a bird, a branch or the noise of a storm.

Their external senses are extremely developed. By means of their internal senses, which are just like ours – memory, imagination, instinct for self-preservation and common sense – they evaluate the vital experiences according to two categories:

- Dangerous situation from which they have to escape, like the proximity of a predator.
- Non dangerous situations, like the flight of a bird, to which they have to get "accustomed."

A horse that has been punished by a man will be negatively reinforced towards him and will try to avoid him because he will regard him as dangerous. Therefore, according to what the horse perceives as positive or negative in its first experiences, it will develop enduring habits or reactions: trust or distrust before positive or negative stimuli. That is why it is very important for the horse to undergo positive experiences with men, with the discipline for which it will be trained and with the corresponding environment. The environment includes: noises, a lot of people, veterinarian examination, fitting of horseshoes, transfer in trailers, and the presence of other animals. When a horse is filled with positive experiences it will live as an adult, it will be better inclined not to categorise them as harmful. If the memory of the first horseshoe is positive, the successive experiences with horseshoes will also be positive. The problem arises when the memory is negative. It is important to bear that information in mind so as to prevent the horse from regarding something as harmful or dangerous when it is not.

Horses can be easily dominated because they are herd animals and genetically prepared to respond to a leader or a hierarchy. In the wild, the herd needs a consistent and reliable leader to live according to the rules of the group. Therefore, in the man-horse relationship, they will try to reproduce the natural relationship with the leader and they will try to respond to men as they would naturally respond to the leader, as long as men know how to exercise that function.

How does the stallion leader or the leading mare exert domination? They do it through movement and direction. Their main language of control is the movement he or she uses to control the movement of the other members of the herd.

According to R. Miller, in a species in which the ability to run marks the difference between life and death, to control that activity is likely to be the most efficient way of establishing leadership. The leader makes some movements and threatening gestures to the submissive ones and in some way, consciously or not, men do the same: when they make the horse move even if the animal does not want to, or when they stop the horse even if the animal wants to keep moving.

Every species has its own communication system which is learned during their social lives. We should try to learn their often subtle body signs, to communicate in a coherent way in their "own language." It is a useful, amusing and functional method that saves time, effort and negative situations.

In the following chapters we will see cases, stories and the detailed foundations of how the horse's mind works and what social rules govern their group life, through a study focused on communication with horses.

CHAPTER I

TAKHI, THE WILD HORSE

The stallion buck, stallions' fight. (English Art – 17th c.)

TAKHI, THE WILD HORSE

*Criollo little horse,
with long breath,
with short gallop
and faithful instinct.*

Modern biology explains that throughout the evolutionary process of horses, a number of lines coexisted. Creationists claim that certain features, such as the number of fingers, come from preexistent information that is activated or deactivated according to the circumstances, together with natural selection which withdraws the unnecessary information. Due to the fact that horses preserve certain physical characteristics such as the hocks – according to some people, the remains of a finger in the interior part of an arm – or the rudimentary metacarpus and metatarsus bones, they can adapt to the different changes that might take place within our planet, such as becoming smaller or larger if circumstances so require it. This great ability to adapt allows them to live with men and to tolerate artificial life and the demands to which they are exposed: a diet that differs so much from the natural one or a life in confinement, even in darkness, something completely strange for a species that needs space, movement and freedom to survive.

The horse is a galloping, herbivorous mammal. Its ability to adapt, its agility and flexibility have probably allowed it to survive varied climates and terrains. These characteristics and abilities are, therefore, a sign of intelligence. This specie´s intelligence can be observed in different aspects of its life.

Primitive tribes have domesticated the horse by means of captivity and artificial selection, obtaining different types of horses in respect of coat, anatomy, temperament and breeds.

Chapter I

Nowadays there are authentic wild horses, such as the Mongolian or Przewalski's Horse with a height of about 130 centimeters, a thick head and a strong neck with erect mane.

There are other horses that live in natural conditions, which are called feral horses. These animals have escaped from the corrals and reservations to live freely, like the Mustangs from the USA, the Brumbies from Australia, the small Iceland horse and the ones that live in different provinces of Argentina. The ethological study of these herds provides helpful information regarding their behavior and abilities.

According to a series of studies, European wild horses were domesticated at the beginning of the third millennium BC in the Russian Steppes, and the smallest subspecies, the tarpan, might have been the founder of the domestic horse family, at least in those altitudes. Apparently, the Przewalski appeared in Western Europe at the prehistoric period and later on the Mongol nomadic people and the Shiites used them as beasts of burden during their invasions to Europe.

Mongol horses were hunted during the 19th c. In 1881, a man called Przewalski (whose origins vary depending on the information source, as he is sometimes described as a Polish geographer or as a Russian explorer) identified a wild species from Mongolia which was impossible for men to capture. They finally managed to capture some specimens to carry out a scientific study and they named that species *Equus caballus*

przewalski, later recognised as one of the oldest ancestors of the domestic horse, that was related to the Steppe Tarpan (*Equus caballus gmelini*), which was declared extinct in 1887.

The inhabitants of the Mongolian Plateau called him "Thakhi", which means wild horse. The first mention of his existence appears in a manuscript from the 13th c.

It is said that Mongolia is the "land of the horses", where children learn to ride a horse at the age of four or five. The takhis are the size of a pony; they are bay or dark grey with a dorsal dark stripe, with a strong complexion and a short and strong back. The coat is thick in the winter and becomes lighter and shiny in summer. The mane is dark brown and stands erect and rigid like that of the zebra, and their legs are striped like the zebra. They are really strong, have 33 chromosomes instead of 32, and are smaller than the modern horse. They have a very wide forehead (a sign of intelligence) and they were gifted with great decision-making skills. Nowadays, there are about 1,500 of these horses living in captivity, some of which are in semi-wild conditions in huge reservations in Canada, China, Germany, the Netherlands and Ukraine, where they are prepared to be reinserted into wild life.

At the Justain Nuruu reservation, located on the Mongolian Plateau, many groups of these horses live freely, after being kept in semi-wild conditions at the climatisation zone. These groups are monitored so as to be sure that they adapt to their new

Chapter I

environment and to get to understand their behaviour. They are constantly studied to determine the number of animals that might survive independently before being released, and have to learn the basic instinctive abilities of survival. Colts who are born in semi-wild conditions, with the least human interference possible, have fewer problems when adapting to the environment. Those who take care of the horses say that it is exciting to see how easily they adapt to the new environment, even when they confront wolves, a moment when adult horses surround the younger ones to make the wolves flee. It is interesting to note that we can still recover species that were thought to be irrecoverable some time ago.

EQUUS MAIN FEATURES

Physical characteristics

- Long, strong and functional spine to develop great speed when galloping in a linear direction.
- Elongated head.
- Eyes set on the side of the head which provide a precise vision to detect predators at any time, even when eating with their heads facing downwards.
- A finger with rudimentary bones.
- Collateral ligaments borne from the hock which allow rigidity and stability in movement and allow it to sleep standing up.
- Good muscular capacity for propulsion movement.
- Big molars to chew and grind grass.
- Mobile, concave ears to capture the widest range and number of noises.
- Very sensitive nostrils and lips, capable of distinguishing different pastures.

- Long, flexible and strong neck.
- Good thoracic capacity.
- Abdomen adapted to support a process of continuous flow of fibrous material. This is the reason why it is so important to maintain the alimentary behavior of horses, because they naturally eat small quantities during many hours so as to be light in case they have to flee.

Mental characteristics

- Highly developed social structure: cooperation, hierarchy and communication.
- Great capacity to detect and flee from predators, thanks to the refinement of its escape reaction.
- Capacity to develop great speed in a short time.
- Shrewdness to survive in different environments.
- Good nutritional adaptation.
- Extremely sensitive skin with helpful body twitching to keep insects away.

According to my criterion, nutritional adaptation and the subtle sensitivity of the skin are part of its mental flexibility. A small and light stomach allows it to run away in case it needs to flee, while a thin or thick but sensitive skin is ideal for a delicate and profound contact, with a good capacity of perception.

Chapter I

Where do horses stand in the animal scale?

- They belong to the animal kingdom
- They are creatures that move for themselves and reproduce sexually.
- They belong to **the chordates (Phylum Chordata)** because they have a spinal cord, to the vertebrate subtype (Subphylum Vertebrata) because the spine is located inside the spinal channel, skull and brain. (Fishes, reptiles, birds and mammals.)

Class: Mammals (Mammalia)

These are the vertebrates who have hair and breast-feed their offspring (elephants, ovines, canines, mice, whales, bovines, caprinae.)

Order: Ungulates (Ungulata)

These are the mammals that have hooves, protective structures of hard corneous tissue at the end of their limbs. This tissue is a tubular material of keratin.

Perissodactyl Suborder (Perissodactyla)

These are the ungulates who have a number of uneven fingers in each limb, while the artiodactyls have an even number of fingers, such as the bovine, the deer and the porcine. Their stomach is simple, without compartments. There are only three families: tapirs, rhinoceros, equines. According to some evolutionist researchers, tapires and rhinoceros are relatives of the equines.

CHAPTER II

HOW DO HORSES COMMUNICATE?

Epigraph: The Fight (Stubbs – 1779)

HOW DO HORSES COMMUNICATE?

*What an excellent horse do we lose!
For want of address
and boldness to manage him!*

PLUTARCH

Equestrian Alexander the Great, Ist c. BC (Unknown author)

A story that has always fascinated me was the story of Alexander the Great and his horse, Bucephalus. I felt attracted to this legend since I was a child and I still think about it, because I believe there is something more in its essence.

Alexander the Great was a general - according to some the greatest of all - who built a vast empire and never lost a battle. The eldest son of Philip II, King of Macedonia, his teacher was Aristotle. He was in battles from a very young age and was king from the age of 20 to 33. According to legend, he asked his father for a horse from Thessalia, since those were the best horses for war. Thus, he obtained the famous Bucephalus, jet black, with a white star on his forehead and a head like an ox; hence his name. Apparently, his elegance and temperament made him outstanding.

Plutarch, in his book *Parallel Lives: Alexander and Caesar*, writes the following:

"Philonicus the Thessalian brought the horse Bucephalus to Philip offering to sell him for thirteen talents. But when they went into the field to try him, they found him so very vicious and unmanageable, that he reared up when they endeavored to mount him, and would not so much as endure the voice of any of Philip's attendants.

Chapter II

> Upon which, as they were leading him away as wholly useless and untractable, Alexander, who stood by, said, 'What an excellent horse do we lose! For want of address and boldness to manage him!'
>
> Philip at first took no notice of what he said; but when he heard him repeat the same thing several times, and saw that he was much vexed to see the horse sent away, 'Do you reproach,' he said to him, 'those who are older than yourself, as if you knew more, and were better able to manage him than they?'
>
> 'I could manage this horse,' replied he, 'better than others do.' And if you do not,' said Philip, 'what will you forfeit for your rashness?'
>
> By Zeus 'I will pay,' answered Alexander, 'the whole price of the horse.'
>
> At this the whole company fell a-laughing; and as soon as the wager was settled amongst them, he immediately ran to the horse, and taking hold of the bridle, turned him directly towards the sun, having, it seems, observed that he was disturbed at and afraid of the motion of his own shadow; then letting him go forward a little, still keeping the reins in his hands, and stroking him gently when he found him begin to grow eager and fiery, he let fall his upper garment softly, and with one nimble leap securely mounted him, and when he was seated, by little and little drew in the bridle, and curbed him without either striking or spurring him. Presently, when he found him free from all rebelliousness, and only impatient to run, he let him go at full speed, inciting him now with a commanding voice, and urging him also with his heels. Philip and his friends looked on at first in silence and anxiety for the result, till seeing him turn at the end of his gallop, and come back rejoicing and triumphing for what he had performed, they all burst out into acclamations of applause; and his father shedding tears, it is said, for joy, kissed him as he came down from his horse, and said,
>
> 'O my son, look thee out a kingdom equal to and worthy of thyself, for Macedonia is too little for thee.'

Alexander and Bucephalus made an extraordinary couple. Together, they built an empire of more than twenty million square kilometers. Such was the love Alexander had for Bucephalus that, when the horse died in battle, at the age of 28, Alexander named the place Bucephala.

The question that came to my mind when I read and re-read this legend was: How did Alexander understand so quickly that he could ride Bucephalus, and that he could do it well? Evidently, he knew the horse's language and he could understand what had happened to Bucephalus. Bear in mind the phrase written by Plutarch: "What an excellent horse do we lose! For want of address and boldness to manage him!" It is worth remembering that the Greeks studied and were well acquainted with nature's laws.

Equine communication is based on a silent body language – made of signs and signals – together with a vocal and odoriferous language. It is a precise language that quickly expresses the horse's state of mind. Horses, being prey animals, are very perceptive, emotional and they have a lot to "say" to each other. Their life as part of a group, just as in human society, entails knowing and abiding by certain social rules that are designed to keep balance and unity for all individuals. In order to stay in balance, they constantly communicate with each other but, since most of this communication is silent, some people ignore it and do not take it into consideration. Some messages seem to be instinctive while others need to be learned: some express a feeling such as joy for being among friends; others are warnings, such as: "we are going somewhere else".

Since every horse expresses itself in its own personal manner, the surrounding circumstances have great effect on it, and not every message is easy for us to understand. Therefore, we need to keep watching and studying them in order to truly interpret their communication system. In every signal exchange there is a lot of information. It is very useful to watch how a herd functions in "silence", either in a pasture, in a breeding establishment or in their natural environment. How do they communicate? How many messages do they exchange? What are those messages? Sometimes, their look is so intense they seem to be saying: "what are you doing?" or, "what do you want?"

We live in a mechanical, noisy, success-obsessed society, in which the value of silence is lost. I think many people lose the chance of understanding horses because they do not pay attention to this. Every good trainer stimulates peace and quietness in order to work with horses. In human beings, it is possible to transmit a lot of information in this state; the mind stays clear and is more receptive because different brain synapses are formed, and the slower forms of thought are activated.

Just as horses constantly try to communicate with each other, they also try to communicate with humans. But, strikingly enough, they learn to read us quickly, with great accuracy and clarity and, more often than not, before we understand them. This is a great challenge for us: to learn to read them. Many people, who are unaware of this great ability of horses to read our language, miss the opportunity of communicating with them because they do not understand their reactions in the presence of tense, excited, anxious or unbalanced people. Being prey animals, horses are capable of detecting, in a split second, the state of mind of people who come near them and, if these people are tense, anxious or scared, they unwillingly tell them that something bad may happen; therefore, they "make them nervous", as it is usually said.

Chapter II

But when communication is calm, they feel at ease. They always try to communicate, even if they do not have feedback but, unfortunately, there comes a point when they get frustrated; their correct language sequence alters and behavior disorders appear, and the worst thing is that some frustrated, ill-treated and misunderstood horses shut themselves away from the world and do not want to "speak" any more, just like children do.

I once worked with a race mare who constantly looked towards the inside corner of the box, her back to the door, shut away from the world, unwilling to communicate with anyone. Even though people called her, she did not reply. The groom moved her to another box with bars that allowed her to be in contact with the mare right next to her. Thus, she spent hours in silent contact with her friend or looking through a small window in one of the corners of the box. As part of the treatment, I included massages, and I spoke a lot to her. As a result, after a couple of weeks, when I got to the stud, I called her, and she waited for me, her head popping out. That was the beginning of her recovery: the moment when she felt the need to communicate again.

A classic example of this "shutting away from the world" is the patient rental horse who lives tired, bored and frustrated, due to lack of care and affection. Once, I had to see a couple of rental horses during an interview. The process of change that took place during the massage was striking, because even though they were indifferent at the beginning, gradually they started to be receptive to someone who listened to them from the other side and, without being extremely expressive, they started showing positive signs.

Indians in my country, like in many other countries, were thoughtful, patient and perceptive when interacting with their horses, who had to be extremely alert when in action. And they were. These animals were highly desired by the enemy army, as their soldiers were unable to make such efficient pairings of horse and man. Soldiers were paid to destroy the natives. For the Indians, life, honour and pride were at stake.

Jose Hernandez, author of *Martin Fierro*, wrote:

When you're riding a mount that's Indian trained
You needn't fear a roll,
La Pucha! And as for doing a bolt
There's none can outpace or outlast his colt,
He doesn't hit it with quirt and spur
But with word-and-hand control.

He handles it softly for a start,
Its neck with his hand he slicks,

He doesn't care what time he'll spend,
He strokes it there for hours on end,
And he only stops when it drops its ears
And neither jibs nor kicks.

Not a single blow he gives it there
With whip or yet with hand;
There's no patienter thing in the universe,
Than the way of an Indian with a horse,
When he's finished with it his every word
The beast can understand.

"Tame" (from Spanish *amansar*) is an Argentinean, *creole* word. They tamed, they neither dominated nor brutally broke, they educated them in a friendly manner.

Horses have a wide range of vocal repertoire with personal sounds, like the whisper of the mare to her foal, an individual sound the latter quickly recognises. As part of their communication system, smell communication is also paramount. When two horses meet, they carefully smell each other in order to decide whether they are going to be friends or not. **(See picture 1)**

Picture taken from the Ministry of Education, Science and Technology web site. Undersecretariat of the Argentine Administrative Coordination.

It is similar to when we shake hands with someone, a ritual by which we perceive whether there is sympathy or not. Therefore, when a horse carefully sniffs a person, he is showing that person exactly that: his interest in meeting him or recognising him. **(See picture 2)** When a horse is taken out from the group and then returned to the pasture, many of his mates come to smell him, as a kind of welcome ritual.

HOW DOES VOCAL COMMUNICATION WORK?

Vocalisations transmit information about their state of mind, which varies depending on the circumstances. In order to understand the meaning of this information, it has to be analysed together with posture. Henry Blake, author of the book *Thinking with Horses*, conducted a thorough analysis of language and found different meanings depending on the vocalisations made.

Chapter II

The horse's most famous vocal sound is the *neigh*, a loud and long sound, made with open mouth. They neigh when they want to communicate their presence, as when they are separated from their herd. A mare, newly arrived from the racetrack, would start a concert of neighs whenever she left her place, as soon as she walked 100 or 200 meters, which could be heard all over the place. Immediately, the answers from all the members of the equine community could be heard, as if saying: "We can hear you, here we are." After a while, when she got used to going out, she no longer needed to tell her neighbors and friends where she was. It is a message of information and search: "Where are you? Is there anyone there?" and it is aimed at keeping contact and tracking all the members of the group. Every neigh has its own personal quality, which the rest identify. For example, when a member of the group is left behind, the mare neighs waiting for an answer, and realises if the answer comes from the member who has moved away. Some stallions, who live loose in their paddocks and from where they can watch the other animals, neigh when there is a lot of movement, as when the mares are taken out of the pasture or when they do not see them for some time, or when the sun starts to fall. Thus, they keep in touch. Some even calm down after neighing.

Horses whisper

When they need closer contact, or when they welcome their close friends (either equine or human) or their foals, horses whisper. This sound is soft, short, deep and pulsating. They make this sound when they feel at ease, as when food arrives or when someone they love arrives. When the mare communicates with her foals, she may whisper to them if they stray too far or to welcome them after a ride. Foals learn to imitate this sound as soon as they are born and they use it when they get up after resting, when they come back running or when they play near their mother. The stallion whispers to the mare during courtship, but this sound is deeper, a bit longer, powerful and pulsating, and he does it at the same time as he shakes his head up and down.

They also squeal

They do so when they need to warn of something or for complaining. For example, when two horses, who are not very close or who are not friends, meet but do not wish to have much contact, they squeal and paw to avoid their private space being invaded. It is a way of avoiding a too familiar contact, as might be the case when a mare is forced to be serviced by a stallion she does not accept. This is not permanent, since I have seen horses who do not know each other, squealing during the first encounters but, as they get more familiar with each other, they stop and become closer every time. Squeals can be short or long and can be heard up to 100 meters away. At an equestrian center I know, there is a jumping mare who, when someone comes near her box, squeals and turns her ears downwards, not completely flat to her head. When I approached her, I discovered her squealing was like a game, like colts' squealing when they play at scaring each other. It is a mare who did not have the chance to practice her language, so language sequences are blocked. Therefore, her way of asking things is a little rough, similar to what happens with those children who are a bit rude seeking contact. Some horses, who spent many years shut away, squeal a lot when they start living loose, until they get used to their new life and become confident as they socialise. They also squeal when fighting or when bucking, if they are upset.

They sometimes snort or puff

They do this when they want to warn against some danger and indicate where that danger comes from. When they snort, they expand their nostrils, inhale deeply, open their lungs, take in oxygen in order to prepare the muscles, and exhale strongly. Stallions puff or snort when they confront another stallion. They also snort when they feel curious about unknown objects, other animals or strangers, and especially when there is a clash between their curiosity and their fear of the unknown. But they can also snort when they feel "very good" while playing.

Some riders say that when they go out to the country to gallop and have fun, their horses snort, just as when they return from the country or after work, especially if the latter has been satisfactory. It is useful to imitate these puffs when working with them in order to improve communication, and it is really good for them! Some even answer back with another puff. They also puff when they are expecting some activity, or when they are loose in the pasture.

Chapter II

> *According to Lucy Rees: "The most dangerous situation in which you can hear a horse **screaming** is when a horse with genuine behavior problems has decided to kill a person."*

They roar when they are angry

Or when they are very scared, like some untamed colts when they are thrown to the ground during the taming process. It is really impressive to hear these colts roaring, since they express a mixture of fear, helplessness and rage. It is a deep, long, highly vibrating sound that expresses an extreme emotional state.

There are other vocalisations that serve to express an emotional state or a great effort. Some examples are groans, whines and grunts, apparently involuntary sounds made during labour, when they get up from the ground, when they yawn, or when they are in pain and, in some horses, when defecating or urinating.

It is a way of releasing tension, like the groan they make after a huge effort like jumping. It is a deep, strong, slightly vibrating sound.

Some foals and some adult horses snore when they are sound asleep, surrounded by their mates who protect them. A friend's mare sighs heavily when my friend greets her after not seeing her for a long time. Others sigh when they are relaxed, when they are bored or when they finish a task.

HOW DO THEY EXPRESS THEMSELVES THROUGH THEIR BODY?

Body posture accurately shows their emotional and health condition. Horses watch and perceive their mates' shapes, in motion or stillness. If they move, they watch the direction of the movement and characteristics: if they eat, drink or sleep. They express themselves with their entire bodies, with such subtleness and precision that even the skin's shivering indicates something.

When a horse gets excited, it tenses its body and rises, indicating to the rest that they should pay attention to some danger. Its entire body is "on the alert", ears pointing to the place which draws its attention, head raised, tail high, muscles active, and with an intense look. When it relaxes, the entire body relaxes. There are different degrees of relaxation; they can have their whole energy "downwards", as when they are bored, sleepy or locked inside stalls, because they do not need to pay attention to anything.

Docile horses also have a downward position, without energy, their ears to the sides or downwards.

Warning or "something new is happening to me" posture

Alarmed horses have their entire bodies in a "warning" posture to be able to decide if they have to run or not and, at the same time, to communicate what should be done. They raise their head towards the focus of attention, their ears raised and active in order to detect the possible origin of danger, their nostrils wide open to smell and snort. The body posture is striking due to its vigor, as they prepare their muscles for action, in high steps; tail raised and curved neck, their senses sharp in order to find out what is going on. The alert posture is meaningful for the rest of the members of the group. If they perceive any danger, they get together to run away; if they do not, they relax.

In **pictures 3 and 4**, we can observe a quarter mile filly during her first work at the round corral. She still does not know what she has to do; therefore, she is tense, her spine stiff and her movements clumsy.

Stallions who show themselves before a mare during courtship, or before another stallion, grow in stature and "dance", displaying their strength and beauty.

How do they express themselves with their tail?

Through their movements and the positions they adopt they produce different signs which, together with their ears, clearly change their surroundings.

Basically, they raise their tail during excitement and they put it down during relaxation. When they are afraid or are very submissive, they put it between their legs. If they feel panic, they swing it to and fro, like an attack warning. But they can also swing their tail when they do not understand what somebody tells them and feel afraid, uneasy or uncomfortable, especially if they are new horses. When it rains or when it is windy you can see them, tail between their legs, against the rain or the wind, in close together groups to keep warm. In **pictures 5, 6 and 7** you can see different attitudes expressing different inner states.

When they are scared, they can defecate several times, or even get diarrhoea, like horses who run or who enter the trailer for the first time. In order to defecate, they must raise their tail. Many situations frighten horses: getting into the jumping area, weaning, being separated from the group. Even bad memories cause them to react with fear and to defecate many times; some horses do it exaggeratedly when they are moved from one place to another for example.

Chapter II

Stallions raise their tail when they want to show themselves. Foals, when they run to play also raise their tail, and adult horses raise it slightly when they are about to move. When I let Jadrift – my mare – loose for the first time on a farm, after being locked inside the racetrack for three years, she first watched the two loose mares and started running very elegantly with her tail raised, showing off entirely. The others, who were already used to the field, welcomed her very calmly. She looked like a city girl strutting along among country girls.

When they get annoyed due to some frustration or conflict, when they are upset or in pain, or when they are bitten by an insect, they swing their tail violently, like a lash. Some do it during their learning or during a physical effort, showing that they feel the effort, the discomfort or the pain.

Mares in heat raise their tail. Their body is relaxed because they have their head and ears relaxed. But the most striking sign is the vulvar winking, which they do by opening and closing the vulva, producing a contrast in colors, together with a secretion that attracts the stallion.

My horse's ears swing to and fro

Ears are very mobile and expressive, and are therefore the best sign of the focus of attention. Their movements transmit visual information which expresses the different states of mind. Due to their muscles, horses can locate the auditory channel at the perfect angle in order to capture every sound.

If the sounds are too deep and sharp, they put the ears backwards, in order to shut the auditory channel and protect the ear. For example, the horses of a club next to an airport are resigned and sort of "asleep". Those sounds are very loud for their keen ear, even though they may get used to them.

Horses' hearing is very keen. Some enjoy the sound of music, singing and soft whistles. A horsebreaker who played classical music in his stable said that, when he stopped playing music, the horses neighed as if they were complaining about its absence. Also, at some clubs where labourers play tropical music, they see that on the days they do not play music, horses miss it, get sad, and change their mood. Maybe it is a series of combined factors that gives stabled horses the feeling of company, activity and communication. It is known that good music creates an atmosphere of harmony.

Basically, horses who are on the alert raise their ears and point them towards the source of attention. Relaxed horses let them loose, indicating attention towards themselves or lack of it. Between these two positions, there are many variations. When they are sleepy, bored or apathetic, their ears are down. Submissive horses have their ears half backwards, except for foals, who raise them at the same time as they open and close their mouth, an inhibiting gesture of adults' aggression.

Mounted horses, who pay attention to the rider and to their surroundings, swing their ears to and fro, pointing towards what they hear; sometimes forward, pointing towards where they are going; sometimes to the sides, bored; sometimes backwards, towards themselves or their riders. Horses who are in tune with their riders have their ears backwards during the entire activity, or most of it, like racing horses who are in tune with their riders. When they pay attention to something behind them, they put their ears backwards without this being a sign of aggression, as when they threaten to become aggressive, they pin them flat against the back of their neck. When they get bored, or when they are not comfortable with their rider, or when they are interested in something else, they get distracted which they show by turning their ears out.

When they are sad, unmotivated or upset by the use of devices which force them to keep their head down (weight aids) and which make them tense and prevent their natural swinging, they swing the ears to the sides, with the auditory channel down, showing boredom. They need to move their head in order to focus their vision; therefore, when weight aids are placed on top of them, hindering this natural movement, they feel really bad, unmotivated, and they do their jobs mechanically, with no art or joy.

The mouth is not just for eating

Their lips are very expressive. The foals open and shut their mouth as a sign of submission, an inhibiting gesture of aggression, which means the same as when puppies lie on the floor, belly up, in the presence of adults. As we saw, they also bring their ears forward and stretch their neck. This gesture may reappear in more submissive horses, if they are afraid of a very aggressive adult or if they are threatened, or in young horses who are alone, such as a two-year-old colt who was alone and called the other horses who passed by during a horseback riding. When we came near, it did the same gesture, because it needed to communicate with the others since it was alone, and therefore felt more defenseless. They stop doing this when they grow up, when they stop being their mother's focus of attention and become part of the mature group, a moment when, like puppies, they start belonging to the group's periphery or start different groups. The ones who are raised in groups tend to stop doing this gesture almost at once, except for the most submissive ones, who continue doing it for a longer time.

When they relax after a moment of tension due to fear, concentration or pain, they make a chewing movement, a movement also made by mounted horses when the reins are slackened. Through these little chewing movements, they release tension, just like when we move our shoulders. Poor cart horses, who are sometimes treated with extreme harshness, do it when the reins are slackened. They also do it when they feel well with a person, another horse or during work, as a sign of contentment, a sort of "I feel good." Encouraging them when they do it is a way of sympathising with them; in a way, you tell them: "I share this feeling" and this is more positive for the relationship.

When they threaten to bite, they show their gums and teeth, and flatten their ears against the back of their neck. Some racing horses, who are ticklish when being brushed, clench their teeth or bite whatever they find, even the person brushing them, this being an action of redirected aggression.

When they are upset, angry, confused or scared due to something unknown, they tense their chin and nose. Like a quarter mile filly who was afraid of getting into a very enclosed round corral (**Picture 10**). During a course, we worked with her so that she could overcome her fear of enclosed places. We created situations of physical invasion to make her get used to stimuli similar to enclosure. We went step by step, until she managed to get into the round corral fearless. You can see her tense nose and mouth smelling the blanket. When she finally understood she was not going to be hurt, she relaxed and chewed, as can be seen in **picture 11**.

When they are ill, exhausted or in deep pain, their mouths fall down; if they show fever or dyspnoea, this sign is accompanied by a flapping at the edge of the nostrils.

In order to understand what horses actually express, we have to observe them as a whole, because each one of them is a unique being who expresses in his/her own personal way. Subtly understanding what happens inside a horse is a matter of training. A mare I assisted looked like she wanted to bite someone, or at least the people who took care of her understood that. When I got to know her, and did not get scared at her mouth movements, I realised she only wanted to play, because she never bit me. These horses are weaned at the age of six months, in full youth, and even though they keep playing in their new group, once they enter the box to get ready to be sold, they start living in a more repressed way. I picture the situation like this: they start living inside the box, they have fewer chances of playing and communicating with their mates. So they want to play with the person who takes care of them. If this person is not sensitive enough, as soon as they start playing with their mouth, this person hits them slightly. And so the prejudice begins: "this one is a biter"…and sometimes, just by playing a little with them, they calm down and feel good.

What is the Flehmen response?

Stallions and some mares and foals exhibit the Flehmen response, an action similar to a smile and part of the olfactory communication. Stallions can identify mares in heat approximately 200 meters away. When the male approaches the mare, he needs precise evidence of receptivity or lack of it. Stallions use the vomeronasal organ, a nose cavity located about 10 centimeters away from the nostril's hole over the soft palate, also known as the Jacobson organ, sensitive to pheromones – sexual identity hormones – in charge of carrying chemical messages of the other animal's sexual, emotional and identity state. In pictures 12-14 we can see a Palomino horse exhibiting this response with his lips.

The mechanism is as follows: they curl the upper lip at the same time as they shut the nostrils, deeply inhaling in order to take the air into the organ. One of the functions of this response is to detect urine's pheromones – mares in heat release pheromones through their urine, indicating receptivity– and investigate unfamiliar but attractive smells, situations in which they try to get as much information as possible. Thus, they regulate social conduct and other activities of social life, such as the creation of hierarchies, maternal behavior and the bond between the mother and her foal.

What are pheromones?

Pheromones are volatile substances present in body secretions; their function is to produce a change in the conduct and the physiology of the receiving animal. They are found in skin, in the coat's fat, urine, faeces, air and sweat. Therefore, when two horses meet, they pay extra attention to the mouth, the flanks and the perineal region. Pheromones transmit information related to identity, state of mind and physiology.

Olfactory communication through these substances is very important during the development of the mare and foal mother-filial bond. When the foal is born, his mother sniffs him and does the flehmen response in order to obtain the particular pheromones of her foal, thus establishing the union bond. Since this union process is paramount for an effective bond, it is preferable not to take out the placenta or wash the foal, because this may affect this part of social communication and cause the mother to reject her own foal.

Everything is about communication; the entire language is designed to keep the group together.

They also exhibit the flehmen response when they smell or taste something unexpected, as when a very curious hackney filly curls her upper lip every time she meets someone new. I think that, when they are interested or feel at ease, they need to deepen the contact in this "chemical" sense. It is possible that some horses need more physical contact, others more chemical and others more vocal contact, just like some people prefer the visual aspect, others the auditory or the kinesthetic, while others prefer a mixture.

Chapter II

In this picture we can see how they relate with others using smell.

How do they express themselves through their nostrils?

Nostrils are also very expressive and mobile. You only need to watch racing horses when they finish running to prove it. If they are scared, tense or if they want to pry, they stretch their nose, open their nostrils wide and stretch the snout, expectant, like when they are inside the box waiting for the owners to come with carrots. Every time they investigate something they stretch their entire snout, like the foals in pictures 15-17, bored inside the corral, showing curiosity.

When two horses meet, they sniff each other carefully; they take their time to get to know each other's smell, because through olfaction, they derive information about the other's identity. We can imitate this first encounter in order to be accepted. It usually works, but I have known horses who prefer a stroke rather than a puff.

A great deal of communication and interaction among horses is produced in an atmosphere of harmony. *Horses are mirrors of the people who surround them or ride them.* People who are aware of this, and who are used to dealing with horses, act very relaxed near them, thus creating a pleasant environment which horses appreciate.

There is ritual contact among horses: mutual cleaning, which has several steps. When they intend to clean another horse, they approach him carefully, relaxing the nose and mouth, paying attention to the other horse's attitude, whether he "wants" to be cleaned or not and to take part in the ritual. If they agree, they clean each other at withers level, where the neck and the back are joined, a spot that is difficult to access themselves. They do this with different techniques: they take their mate's skin, stretch it and release it, or they make a movement from one side to the other, rubbing or pinching the skin. **(See pictures 18 and 19).**

We have seen that when they get excited they open their nostrils wide in order to get as much information as possible. They wrinkle their nose when they want to strongly pry into some object that draws their attention, or when they are angry and do not wish to communicate or be invaded in their physical space. As they do this, they put their ears flat against the neck, put on a "bad" face and stretch their eyes and face.

They express so much with their head!

When they threaten, they move their head forward and upward, stretching their neck, their ears flat against the back of the neck, showing their teeth. If the threat is more serious, they stretch their entire body and play "bad", as if they were saying: "Beware, I will attack you".

Soft contact

One night I was seeing to my mare's foal and, at a given moment, I felt a soft push on my right shoulder from her mouth. It was a sign of "I'm here, you're taking care of my foal". Horses who are friends communicate with each other in this soft way in order to move each other, know how they are, or clean each other and they also do it with us if they trust us. With this gesture they confirm trust, like the mare in **picture 21**, who took a course to learn how to trust. In **picture 20** we can see another situation of confirmation of trust through this soft contact, even with willingness to play.

Many horses, especially during summer, try to rub their head against us when we remove their headstall, because perspiration bothers them; sometimes they even shake their head angrily, to get rid of insects or dust after rolling over. Other times, they shake their head out of frustration when they do not get something they want, or to get attention, which I observed in a group of mares who live together. When the owner approaches they all want to get her attention, and the one who does not achieve her goal shakes her head as if saying: "Here, Sevillana" or "Here, Jazmín". When they feel discomfort in the mouth, they can abruptly shake their head upwards and backwards and even do this several times. It is possible to see how some very experienced animals get upset when a new horseman does not interpret the signals correctly.

Foals, colts and young horses are naturally curious about the world and stick their heads into every object or attractive place they see, in order to get to know everything.

Chapter II

The neck is beautiful

The neck is very flexible and mobile. It is useful to see it as part of the overall animal's posture. When they are excited they raise it. If they have to protect themselves from a blow in the head without moving back, they move the neck to one side. They stretch it when prying or reaching out for something or someone. **(Picture 23)**

Stallions wave their neck to and fro and stretch it with their heads down, in order to throw or move the others away. An acquaintance of mine has an Arabian stallion who is used to playing with his dogs. It is amazing to see how the stallion chases them, waving his neck to and fro, trying to look angry, while the dogs pretend they are predators. Once they are satisfied, the game is over. They never hurt each other. When I took my mare to be serviced by Antonio, a Spanish stallion, I let her loose in his paddock and he began to follow her. That day she was no longer in heat, therefore she was not very willing to establish friendship with him. So the stallion, who was very calm and adult, let her eat grass without letting her out of sight. At a given moment when both were on the same line of communication, eight meters away from each other, he put his ears down, stretched his neck and, waving it, approached her in two gallops, as if saying: "It's OK, stay here, but this is my place". Both remained calm, eating their grass, each one in their own spot. What surprised me was how he accepted the mare's rules and, at the same time, how he set his own. This stallion's daughters, who have lived with their mother since they were born, run after dogs waving their neck with their ears flat against the back of their neck.

This horse is a dancer!

Leader stallions or mares manage the rest of the group through movement and direction, but what does this mean? It means they move the ones that do not want to move or stop the ones who want to move, and they also point to the rest of the group the direction to be followed. In a group of horses we can see that when a horse wants to get in the way of another one, he stops and moves to and fro in front of the latter, preventing him from moving along.

There is a very specific contact between the stallion and the mare at the point of the encounter - the shoulder - a spot where the stallion stimulates the mare; the mother mare gets in touch with her foal; or friends among themselves. To massage insecure, uneasy, scared horses in that spot is very useful since we are reminding them of their natural contact. My mare and some of my regular patients usually lean themselves lightly against my shoulder when they want, seek or need more contact.

Picture 1: Carlín and Greta introduce each other.

Picture 2: Greta during the trust course. She sniffs at me so as to reinforce her trust in me.

Pictures 3 and 4: This filly is scared during her first day in the round pen.

Picture 5: Arab horse during a performance. He looks startled because he is in an unknown place with unknown people.

Picture 6: Greta is mounted during a course. She starts moving, swings her tail, but also feels uncomfortable. She does not know the rider. The rigid spine and neck are signs of distrust.

Picture 7: These horses are calm, but a little upset by mosquitoes.

Picture 8: This beautiful palomino colt could not bear the chute. He was trained to overcome that fear. His ears clearly show his inner state: the left one is in contact with me; the right one with the environment and other people, a sign of divided attention.

Picture 9: "What is this?" Notice the chin, nostrils and ears pointing towards the object that calls his attention.

Picture 10: The filly needs to sniff the blanket and become familiar with it, that is why she stretches her muzzle.

Picture 11: When she relaxes, she chews.

Picture 12, 13 and 14: Photo sequence that shows the Flehmen response. The mechanism involves the curling of the upper lip and closing the nostrils, deeply inhaling to carry air to the vomeronasal organ.

Picture 15: "What's up?"

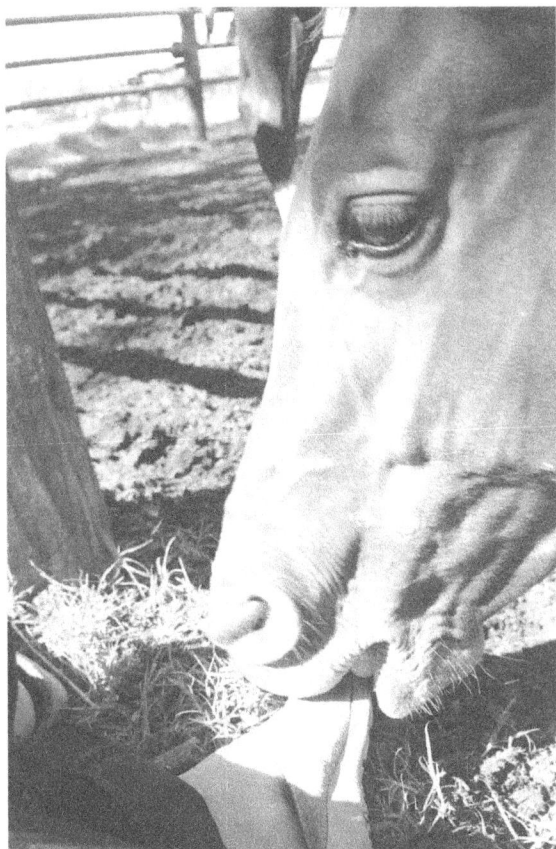

Picture 16: "There are so many things to sniff around. I wrinkle my lips and nostrils increase sensitivity."

Picture 17: "I have to sniff everything to be prepared for when I become a grownup. I like this bag."

Picture 18: The horse gently approaches and chews. Do you want me to lick you?

Picture 19: The other horse agrees and mutual grooming begins.

Picture 20: "I like your hand, I'd like to play"

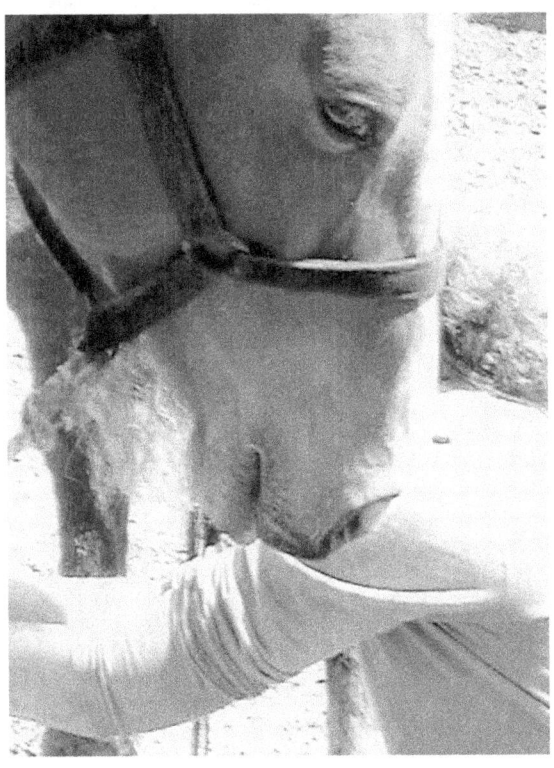

Picture 21: "I find this contact interesting".

Picture 22: During mutual grooming, horses slightly touch each other. In this picture, we can see the way they press certain acupuncture points that relax them.

Picture 23: "Don't go. I'd like to meet you!" Carlín focuses on Greta's point of shoulder, who is reluctant to make contact and turns her head away. Both flex the neck towards their focus of attention.

The croup

There is a very harmful prejudice for horses and for some people who do not know them but want to know them, which is: "You have to be careful because horses kick." Unfortunately, this prejudice, which does not specify under which circumstances horses kick, is very difficult to change at a social level.

Usually, horses kick when they are defending themselves or after warning that they are upset, and have not been listened to. They also do it when playing or when they try to keep insects away. So let us see what it means when horses show their croup: it is a kicking threat. It is true that horses which are hard to grab show their croup. I have dealt with horses who showed their croup when I was about to grab them, but I already knew that they had not been well treated, and I understood that they were simply defending themselves, so I just stood in a spot from where I could dominate them. Thus, I could easily grab them. But it is worth mentioning this: if we are with children or people who are not familiar with horses, we must explain to them **why they should not stand behind a horse**. I point this out so that there is no confusion. It is correct to tell children and people who do not know about horses not to stand behind the hindquarters. But it is also important to explain to them why.

Hooves and legs

Horses, by nature, will *always* try to avoid conflict. But if they have to defend themselves they always warn us through signs that grow in intensity: they show their croup; if they are not listened to, they raise their hoof as a second warning and only after that will they kick. They not only do so out of fear or anger, but also out of annoyance, nuisance or tickling, or when they are bothered by insects.

Some horses with very thin skin or those who are very temperamental get particularly upset with insects and kick against the floor to keep them away. People used to dealing with them firmly scold them or push them with their hands, to prevent them from kicking.

We have seen that horses squeal when they do not want others to come very close, or when they do not want to be invaded in their personal area; often they will stretch one hoof at the same time, as if saying: "don't come too close to me."

Not long ago, a new horse came to a field. This horse went to rest during the summer and was released next to the stallion's paddock, but between the two paddocks there is an electric fence, one meter away from them. The approach and separation ritual sequence happened like this: the new one, let us call it *Negro*, came near the stallion, who "showed off" and squealed at him. *Negro* squealed back and both rose

Chapter II

their hoof indicating: "keep away". Little by little, as they started smelling each other, and even though the stallion kept showing off, he gave in. Since *Negro* was castrated, the squealing and the pawing ceased until they could smell each other peacefully. After a while, both continued eating some meters away from each other. This ritual only lasted for a few minutes.

Horses also paw in other circumstances, such as when they are frustrated because they are tied up and cannot reach an object; when they cannot eat; or when they are curious. They even do it while eating, to move the soil and remove the grass, and before rolling to prepare the field. Also, many horses who live shut away do it, in anticipation of the moment when they will be fed. Some very anxious horses stretch their hooves while eating. I have seen this sign in racing and jumping horses, when they are inside the box and when they eat grains outside. I think that, since they got used to eating in a hurry (they only eat twice a day), even though they are loose afterwards, they still have this feeling of: "at last, the food has arrived."

Horses in the wild eat for approximately 16 hours a day, and do it quietly. However, in the usual artificial conditions, where their eating habits are not taken into consideration, they get used to eating in a hurry when food comes, because they have a feeling of fasting due to the information sent by the receptors located in their stomach.

But I have seen my two-and-a-half-year-old filly repeating this hoof stretching gesture, which she learnt from her mother, when she went to live in a new field inside an already formed herd, where she started belonging to the periphery and where she found more rivalry. Before that, she lived in a big field and had her little family made up of another horse, her mother and herself. There she was the favorite and did not have problems of rivalry.

How do they threaten?

Horses have learned to avoid conflict –it is one of their intelligent mechanisms– in order to survive. Why? Because without conflict they save energy. In social life, there may be situations of rivalry due to hierarchy. Therefore, social animals have had to develop signals of threat or defense. Some authors state that there is the aggressive threat or attack and the defensive threat. Threats have a sequence of signals that in most cases go from the mildest to the strongest, except for horses that have been ill-treated or untamed and wild horses under a lot of pressure, who can attack without warning.

- *Aggressive threat or attack*: They intentionally attack the other –horse or person–, bringing their head forward. This behavior can be observed in strong alpha leaders,

or in overcrowded situations when horses are very angry, with little space to move around and heavy competition over food and water.
- *Defensive threat*: They defend themselves from a potential attack from another animal or person, usually showing their croup first. It may turn into a defensive attack if it is the only way of getting rid of an enemy (like a mosquito!) or if the sequence of warnings was not understood. Most threats carried out by horses to people are done in this defensive manner.

How do other horses respond to threats?

If the threatened horse is of less hierarchy, it submissively leaves, its ears slightly backwards or downwards to the sides. The first one to turn around in a fighting threat is the one who accepts the other's leadership. The submissive animal puts his tail between his legs, avoids visual contact, retreats and plays being innocent, as if saying "I didn't do it."

Submission is biological in horses. They learn social coexistence rules and abide by them, since this assures them group life. This gives them security, more food, contacts and the possibility of surviving as a species, particularly for those genetically able. If, within the herd, a young animal behaves disrespectfully with the other members of the group, the leading mare will punish him by moving him away from the group and in this case he will try to come back, as he will feel his life threatened. In order to come back, he will perform very precise signals of regret and submission, which will be interpreted by the mare, who will determine when he will be able to return. What are these signals? Approaching the mare, giving her his ear - that is swinging it in her direction - chewing and putting his head down, as if saying: "I want to come back, I'm sorry." When she allows him to come back, she takes care of him and cleans him carefully. It is worth mentioning that there is no tyranny in the leader, even if it is the male, whose function is to keep the mares in the herd and serve them, moving away the fillies who are old enough to be served by another male, and keeping away intruders and colts who can serve other mares; or the wise mare, whose function is to point the direction the group must follow, the moment when they should move and respect the rules.

Usually, stallions avoid fighting, because if they fight, someone will get hurt and will have less chance of survival. Therefore, it is common that the youngest or less experienced accept the leadership of the older or more experienced and leave.

Despite what is shown in movies or despite some experiences in breeding facilities where stallions do not lead a natural life horses, and stallions in particular, are usually peaceful, because they naturally prefer peace and quiet. If they are not excited or

Chapter II

frustrated due to lack of communication and contact, from which they suffer when they are shut away, they are usually peaceful. It is only in exceptional circumstances, such as lack of territory or food, when their behavior is modified.

One student, called Maria Florencia Godoy, came to this conclusion after a course: "It is necessary to learn how to read horses from their body language, so vast and logical, seen from the perspective of their evolutionary history and their prey condition. Thus, it is necessary to closely observe horses within herds and their interaction. They are not the ones who have to understand our codes, we are the ones who must interpret and imitate their language when communicating with them. Evidence of this is the relationship they established with Indians, based on the interpretation of signals, imperceptible for impatient and unobservant people."

Another interesting summary after a course was made by an elementary schoolteacher, dancer and body therapist, Analia Sragopian, who expressed: "Being able to feel the horse so close through contact was very intense, and I felt a very powerful connection between us; I never thought I would go through something like this; I was deeply moved." It is worth mentioning that this person is not used to being with horses but is used to being with children and she connects with them with her own body, in a harmonic way. Even though she is not what we would usually call "a horse person" she listens, observes and perceives.

CHAPTER III

HORSES HAVE BRAINS AND FEELINGS

Horse bath (Sorolla – 1909)

Is it a steed that has just passed before my eyes or is it a falling star that has just crossed rapidly like a flash of lightning, ignited by the storm? The dawn lent him its disc as a veil and ran away with it since it suited him marvellously. Whenever he runs it is because he thinks the dawn comes to claim the loan; but the dawn does not catch him. When he lunges at the enemy, the morning stars get tired of following him and the clouds lose track of him...
BEN ABI-I-HAYTAN, from Sevilla

*Galloping arab stallion,
Rebecca Lehmann*

WHY THIS TITLE?

Because some people who are in contact with horses or other animals seem not to understand or think that animals have a brain that works with its own characteristics - call it animal characteristics - equal to our animal characteristics, that include feelings, emotions or, to put it in scientific terms, animal passions.

Saint Thomas Aquinas investigated the functioning of animal passions in his study of mans' soul. These passions are joy, sadness, hope, despair, fear, boldness, courage and anger, with its different varieties. When describing a horse which does not look well, a lot of people say: 'He seems sad, subdued, indifferent' This means that, unconsciously, they describe an animal with feelings. Maybe, when they later speak about it, they deny it because they cannot accept it in their logical or rational thoughts. However, the fact that they deny it does not mean it does not exist.

According to Saint Thomas, we share the same sensory and vegetative potential with animals but we are differentiated from them in that we possess rational potentiality, that is to say, our intelligence with its own faculties. Vegetative potential corresponds to vegetables. So humans possess the three potentials: vegetative, sensory and rational; while animals possess two: sensory and vegetative; and vegetables only vegetative potential.

We breathe, grow, nourish, move, feel, perceive, generate and pry into the world through the sensitive potential. Horses also function at that level with their sensory potential.

Chapter III

What are the functions of these potentialities in the case of horses? What are they for and in what way can we understand them better? Their potential is divided into two: sensory and vegetative, the sensory, according to Saint Thomas, being the closest to man's rationality.

VEGETATIVE POTENTIAL

It is formed by:

- **Nutritional** faculty: its function is the nutrition of the body.
- **Augmentative** faculty: foals grow and achieve their ultimate size which they keep during adulthood.
- **Generative** faculty: the goal is the preservation of the species by means of reproduction. This faculty is the highest one because it implies communicating with another. The previous faculties serve the individual.

SENSORY POTENTIAL

Involves two types of activities: cognitive and appetising.

Cognitive activity

This takes place through external and internal senses.

External senses:

- Sight
- Taste
- Hearing
- Smell
- Touch

Through sensations, horses apprehend the qualities of an object: colour, flavour, sound, heat and cold.

Internal senses:

- Memory
- Imagination
- Instinct
- Common sense

Internal senses use the information perceived by the external senses.

Memory

This is the ability to retain, recall and recognise past experiences. The foal is not born with fear of predators, however, when her mother and the herd run away at the presence of a predator, the foal retains that information in its memory.

From the mechanical point of view, both human and animal memories depend on a material memory located in the nervous system. However, if we take into account the vitalist referents - Saint Thomas - together with the hypothesis of formative cause, which will be developed in the next chapter, we should also consider the morphic resonance hypothesis to comprehend memory in its different forms, the conscious and the unconscious

Imagination

This retains the qualities of a body that is not present, like the rider of the horse. The animal has the rider in mind, although the person is not permanently with him. This is a representative faculty by which an image of the absent body is preserved with its sensory qualities that are captured by the external senses and integrated by common sense: visual, audible, tactile and gustative. In turn, it combines the images preserved, a capacity called creative imagination, inherent to men and some animals or populations that mutate. An example is the case of a horse who adapts something he has been

Chapter III

Horses roll over to stretch the spine, remove insects and to get the smell of the group.

taught and uses it in a different circumstance than the original one. Like a lipizzan stallion trained at school, who goes round the box bucking, to show off in front of other stallions.

Instinct

In man this is called cognitive faculty. It's function is to distinguish between what is dangerous and what is not. The horse, being a prey, knows he has to run away from the wolf or a huge feline because they are their predators.

Instinctive actions might be defined as the different behaviours that species have in an invariable way and with certain characteristics. These actions are as intrinsic

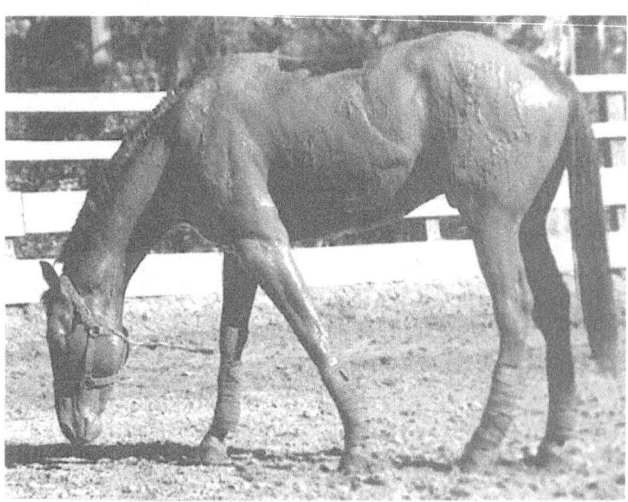

It is natural to roll over. This mare has just finished playing polo, she rolls over, stretches, rubs her skin, gets a mud bath and, most important, resumes the smell of her group.

to animals as their physical appearance. They are always related to the environment. Since animal behaviour is determined to a great extent by the environment where they live, it is possible to infer the structure of their environment by means of their behaviour.

Common sense

This processes diverse qualities at the same time. It is a sort of conscience of the senses, capable of processing all the information together. The main characteristic is that it distinguishes sensations of different nature (such as taste from colour), to integrate them through perception.

In short, the cognitive function is the responsibility of the external senses (sight, taste, hearing, smell and touch) and the internal senses (memory, instinct, imagination and common sense).

Appetising activity

The other function of the sensory potential is appetite, which is divided into concupiscent and irascible. These are emotional movements that are produced because of the beneficial content of an object, the proximity or the existence of a certain difficulty to come closer to it or obtain it. For example, desire. *Desire* is an emotional movement that makes people value an object or an action as beneficial when the object or action is absent. When can we observe this? When a foal moves to get closer to another one in order to play: it runs around the other, inviting it with the intention of playing and the other clearly understands this. Before the movement, desire is necessary. When it succeeds, when it attains its goal, it feels joy because the desire is satisfied - in this case, the desire to play. But when it does not achieve its goal, sadness appears manifested as frustration. This is seen in horses who are locked up for hours and do not communicate with others. After a long time they get frustrated and move away to the darkest place in the box with their croups facing the door as if saying: "I have no interest at all in anything." They have tried so many times to communicate without success that they finally shut themselves away.

Like the race mare I described in a previous chapter. When they called me to treat her, the groom described her as follows: "when she got to the stud, she was fluffy and bright, but now she is skinny, sad, indifferent with dull hair, opaque." She has run pretty well, winning the first race. I went to see her; she was in the box, against the wall at the back, indifferent to everything surrounding her, staring at a closed angle. That state of sadness and apathy was sometimes accompanied by a bad humour because she got irritated when she was cleaned or examined by other veterinarians. But there was a detail: when she went out to train, her humour changed completely and she was easy to handle. Part of her treatment consisted of putting her in a box with windows and bars between walls with a friend by her side. In a few weeks, this simple change modified some of the behaviour symptoms, because during those days when I got to the stud and called to her, she waited, popping out her head. She spent a lot of time next to the bars, in contact with the neighbouring mare and each day it was easier to give her a massage without irritating her. So as not to irritate her within the box, I put into practice a leadership role which modified her attitude. The main issue with this mare is that she felt insecure inside the box because she could not run away. Outside the box, she felt better because if it was necessary, she could do it. This is a good example of sadness and its consequences.

Back to passions, just like desire exists, the opposite does: aversion, which means rejection. When do horses feel aversion? When they regard the object or the action as something harmful or useless. Horses feel aversion, for example, to predators, to people who ill-treat them and to medicine with a bad taste. Companies have had to manufacture palatable medicines because otherwise horses do not ingest them. The mare is also capable of regarding a situation as harmful, in case she has to punish a foal who misbehaves.

Therefore horses, just like humans, naturally desire what is beneficial or useful to them and reject or feel aversion to what is harmful or useless. They are happy when they have what they need or do what makes them feel good or attain a goal; and they grow sad when the opposite happens.

As a rule: they desire what makes them feel good and reject what makes them feel bad. These emotional movements might be observed in a herd or in our own horses, as long as they are healthy and in a suitable place. If there are obstacles that prevent them from attaining their desired object, then contrary emotional movements arise: anger, fear, boldness. These movements appear even in subtler situations; for example, a riding horse got angry with itself every time it knocked the hurdle over. When a horse defends itself from a predator, it uses anger to overcome fear and to save its life. This is exactly what an Asturian pony did when he was attacked by a wolf in the Villaviciosa mountains, in Asturias. His owners named him "Lupito" because, although it was very young when it was attacked, it managed to get rid of the wolf and save its life, probably with help from the herd. It is very tame but, evidently, it could use anger efficiently.

Emotional movements have an effect and might be observed in the body. For example, fear, stress and any other warning signs are accompanied by tachycardia and mydriasis. Evidently, pain in the body affects the mood and *vice versa*. Often, when you treat a horse and ask questions to his owner, he says: "He's been reluctant or apathetic for a long time and he doesn't vault as he used to." Body and mood cannot be separated.

Besides passions or emotional movements, the appetising function is also characterised by the locomotive or locomotory potential, determined by the sensitive disposition: getting close or fleeing. Getting close to the good. Fleeing from the bad. A horse who refuses to jump is rejecting something: maybe it feels pain or fear, or rejection for being mishandled. This knowledge allows us to observe in detail and prevent a problem in advance. Animals always make an effort to communicate with us; we are the ones who need to learn how their communication system works and listen to their subtler signs.

Babieca[1], the Cid Campeador's[2] horse, despite its name, had shown itself to be extremely intelligent. The story goes that when Cid Campeador died and his warriors still had to confront the enemy, his wife, who knew that the vision of this man over his horse was so impressive for the opponents, suggested that they tie her husband's corpse to the horse.

And so they did and finally won the battle. Evidently, Babieca knew what to do, even without his rider. After this battle, nobody rode him again and he died two years later. The story continues to be told and sung by Spanish minstrels, even a hundred years later. If that is not a sign of intelligence, then what is it?

WHAT IS THE HORSE'S NERVOUS SYSTEM LIKE?

Let us take a brief look at the horse´s nervous system. This summary is aimed at knowing and understanding how the learning process works, where memory is located and how and where some answers are produced.

Structure of the nervous system from a functional point of view:

- Central nervous system (CNS), peripheral nervous system (PNS) and autonomic nervous system (ANS).
- The CNS is formed by the encephalon or brain and the spinal cord.

---

1 Babieca: stupid in Spanish.
2 Rodrigo Díaz de Vivar was known as El Cid Campeador, a Castilian nobleman, a military leader and diplomat who, after being exiled, conquered and governed the city of Valencia in the 11th c. He became chief general of Alfonso VI, and he fought against the Moors.

Chapter III

- The PNS is formed by the spinal nerves, which emerge from the spinal cord, and by the cranial nerves, which emerge from the encephalon.
- The ANS is formed by the sympathetic and parasympathetic systems. This system controls involuntary movement and visceral functions.

The yawn is a sign of relaxation and responds to a sign of the nervous system.

Central nervous system

The brain is located in the cranial cavity and has different areas associated with different functions. It analyses the information obtained through the senses and interconnects the functions of conscience and intelligence activities such as learning, memory and imagination. Sensations that come from the external senses arrive in the cortex where they are evaluated.

The frontal area of the brain is formed by overlapping layers. The neocortex is the outer layer of grey substance formed by neuronal bodies that process information. It is a folded layer with an undulating shape where the processing of images and vision takes place. When we say that the cortex takes part in the intelligence process, we are referring to the capacity of association of ideas and logical and deductive reasoning. Horses have the ability to associate but not to establish judgments based on reflections. Their function is not reflection, *that's what human beings are for!*

Under the cortex, we find the white substance formed by axons (that look like light wires) that come and go, carrying information from various places to the brain cortex. The brain cortex is a small part of the right and left hemispheres of the brain, each of which works with messages that come from the opposite side. More deeply, the brain hemispheres have subcortical areas that are extremely important in multiple processes of transmission of information, and analysis of that sensory information from the world that surrounds us. Horses do not have a great ability to make cross-references between both hemispheres. What does this mean? It means that when they learn something from one side, they do not pass it directly to the other, like humans do and, for that reason, they have to learn everything from each side. An example that illustrates this situation is that of a racehorse who used to leave in a hurry while he was mounted from the left side because that was the information he received while living at the racetrack: "Be mounted and leave in a hurry." One day, he was mounted from the right side and stayed completely still. Gradually, he learned to stay still even when he was mounted from the left side. He was first mounted from the right and then from the left.

The interesting thing about this experience is that, although they find it difficult to make cross-references, the horse quickly learned to stand still because it was taught to understand the situation: being mounted could be pleasant. Maybe when the experience is performed quickly from one side then the other, as it's mind associates everything that occurs in that situation - the fact that being mounted could be agreeable - helps erase the memory: "I have been mounted, I have to run."

Good trainers recommend working with two reins and handling from below and from both sides because it is useful for the physical development and mental equilibrium of the horse. As we saw with the previous example, if the horse is taught from the same side every single time and then you ask something from the opposite side, the animal might react as if he has never experienced that. Similarly, if he has lived a traumatic experience from one side he might react with fear on that side, but not on the opposite.

Those who are unaware of that mechanism blame the horse for his attitudes when those reactions are actually consistent with the way his mind works.

Midbrain or thalamus

There is a group of cells that form a ring called limbic system which is located in the centre of the midbrain. This centre automatically regulates the body functions and the olfactory sense, is related to the affective functions, feelings (such as pain and pleasure) and is also part of the learning function. Apparently, the size is similar to that of man, a sign of how emotional and sensitive horses are. There are other areas of the brain that monitor nutrition, temperature and the union between body and brain, and also a part

Chapter III

of the reproductive behaviour or generative potential, the goal of which is to generate and communicate, that is why stallions are so communicative.

The spinal cord

This is located in the vertebral column and is protected by it and coordinates the vegetative functions. Which are these functions? Those that do not need volition, like the regulation of vital and body involuntary functions such as breathing. It is located in the white substance of the brain. This substance is composed of a number of structures that process sensitive information; bundles of nerve fibres that transport information to the processing centres; and connections between structures. Information is processed within the neuronal nuclei located in the grey substance and is transported by the axons of the neurons.

Peripheral nervous system

This is formed by an extended network of nerves and ramifications with different functions. It is composed of an *afferent system* and an *efferent system*. The former transports the sensitive information to the brain and the spinal cord. The latter sends out the motor information from the upper encephalic centre and the spinal cord towards the muscles and peripheral organs to produce a reaction, either a movement or a glandular secretion.

The main function of the nervous system is to collect sensitive information from the whole organism through its peripheral nerves and take it to the spinal cord and the brain in order to process the information in the mechanism of thought and memory and produce, in turn, the motor response, sending signals to the muscles or other internal organs. Therefore, it is a motor-sensitive system.

Process dynamics – The reflex arc

This is the basic functioning unit at the medullary level and produces a motor response to a sensitive stimulus. The system depends on the input and output of messages.

The sensitive afferent neuron transports a nervous impulse from the peripheral receptors (receptors of pressure, pain and proprioception) to the spinal cord where it synapses with a second motor, efferent neuron that produces the motor response. The reaction is immediate, short-lived and quite specific, such as the muscle twitching to defend itself from a mosquito, the blinking produced as a result of a bright light or the sneeze caused by irritation of the respiratory tract.

There are simple reflex responses to certain stimuli, like the withdrawal reflex to a painful stimulus – flexor reflex – the stretch reflex which makes the muscles contract when they are stretched – myotatic reflex – and more complex spinal reflexes. This is a very precise system and it is also formed by interneurons that are found among the aforementioned neurons. There is a group of reflexes that control body movement. These reflexes make the correct muscles synchronise in order to keep the horse standing or make it move. Most reflexes are produced with little intervention from the brain or the memory. Senses capture the message and transport it to the spinal cord where the answer is produced, without the participation of the brain in the analysis. If the horse perceives a suspicious movement with the angle of the eye, it does not wait, it reacts and flees. It is useful to remember that the most important thing for a horse is survival. This is the basic thought.

Efficient training aims at weakening reflex reaction, such as a fear reaction that might be produced by a certain movement similar to a predator about to attack, which horses perceive with their lateral vision. Reflexes are developed by stimulus repetition that provokes an increase in tolerance and, at the same time, a decrease in the response. This process is called habituation and it will be developed in the chapter devoted to learning.

The cerebellum

The cerebellum is an area that has evolved pretty well in horses compared with other species. Obviously, a prey animal needs equilibrium, balance and coordination in order to survive; therefore, it is logical that the cerebellum, which controls locomotion, balance, muscles and limb coordination, is fully developed. There are different types of cells depending on the function they perform: some register head movements, while others register position. These cells send the brain information to work with on coordination and balance when the head moves or changes position.

These are the basic functions of the cerebellum:

- Locomotion, balance, coordination of the muscles and limbs; balance and coordination of the movement, and head position.
- Certain body therapy techniques used with babies and adults are also used to improve balance and equilibrium in animals who have suffered from severe disorders, trying to rebalance lost patterns of movement, and also basic drives of the movement of the cerebrospinal fluid. It is possible to influence the brain from certain specific movements from different parts of the body.
- Some people claim that horses are not intelligent because, if they were, they would not allow people to mount them. These people use inaccurate comparisons to make that conclusion, because in order to evaluate other beings, it is necessary to

know what they have been created for and what their instruments and goals are. Horses are intelligent enough to live in their own environment and to perform their horses' functions. That is why they are horses. Their actions and reactions are supremely tuned to their survival. Horses who live "imprisoned" have their intelligence and fine sensitivity repressed, they can neither communicate nor carry out the activities of their own species, and their reactions are sometimes rude and they even develop displacement behaviours. They manifest reactions and disorders that some people might regard as foolish.

In order to jump, horses need equilibrium, coordination and balance

Dr. Worthington says that: "Even though the brain is not big enough, the cerebral cortex is, and that is a sign of their learning ability. Some brain experts believe that the more gyrus in the brain, the more intelligence. Given the importance of the animal's size, the horses' brain is relatively small in relation to the body volume. So, according to this theory, every gyrus of the cortex will only serve the purpose of thinking how to survive and there will be little space for reasoning, resolution of problems and creative thinking. However, the equine's cerebral cortex is exceptional and, as the size and complexity are also exceptional, we may ask ourselves: How much do we really understand of what takes place there and what is the real potential of the brain?" I think this question that Dr. Worthington asks herself is essential and compels us to continue studying the horse.

People who work with natural horsemanship methods, work with the horse's mind, with the intention of keeping it "sound", not traumatised, so as to get intelligent, cooperative, easy to handle and easy to train horses. Horses with sound minds perform better than those that are traumatised. The fact that they have an emotional centre with a similar size to that of humans is something that leads us to new questions because it supports the idea that horses are able to feel strong and deep emotions.

HOW DOES MEMORY WORK?

Memory is part of the internal senses and part of the sensitive potential. Its function is to *retain*: register and store ; *evoke* and even *recognise* memories from useful experiences together with the act of discernment that the instinct carries out. It might be compared with a "hard disk" which registers past experiences and useful decisions that form the referents for a future life. According to different research, memory would be located within the DNA of some brain cells, in electric currents.

Register: Data is perceived, understood and stored in the short-term memory which has little capacity. For this reason, if this data is not reconfirmed by constant repetition, it will be replaced with more important or up-to-date data, which passes to the long-term memory.

This data is part of the internal senses; therefore, the information is recovered from the unconscious to the conscious through sensitive memory and imagination. The system is very efficient and depends on how good the data has been codified during accumulation.

Accumulation: The ability to remember is generally considered a sign of great

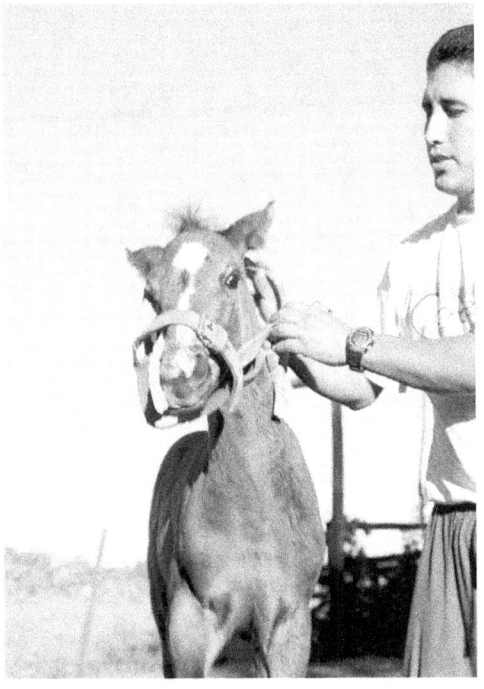

Positive experiences are remembered forever when they are stored in the long-term memory.

intelligence. Those who have spent a great amount of time with horses agree that they have an excellent memory for the information that has been properly stored. Not only in respect to what they have learned, but also in respect to people with whom they have established affective bonds. A colleague told me he had treated a horse for a few months. A few years later he found the horse in another place and when he called him by his name, the horse whispered a welcoming sound. The interesting thing about this anecdote is that when this professional treated the horse, he saw him once a week or every two weeks. It was not his horse, but he had established a bond with the animal. *Horses do not forget.*

Evocation: As we saw in the previous story, horses recognise people, places and even other horses after a long period of time of not seeing them. Every good horse trainer or rider knows that a lesson well learned will stay in their memory forever.

For a prey animal, a mistake might cost it its life; therefore young animals need to learn quickly those situations that are dangerous. Knowledge about predators marks the difference between life and death. In a similar way, knowledge of territory, food and water sources and a precise memory of that information are part of this long-term memory which will guarantee the survival of the group. They are efficient in choosing the right place to live, and every member of the group is capable of remembering field details.

An intelligent and sensitive trainer knows how to use the excellent memory of the horse to train it correctly, because he knows that if the animal experiences the training as something traumatic it will remember and might become a disturbed horse in the future.

But for a bad experience to be remembered, it has to be constant and repeated, except if it is a very traumatic experience such as an accident (for example the one the horse from *Lord of the Horses* suffered) or an abusive situation. Most information becomes permanent when it is reinforced by repetition during training.

A good example of how memory works is that of a three-month old filly on whom they put a little muzzle with the halter. In a moment, she ran away and the labourer let her loose so as not to frighten her. When he stepped on the halter, she got scared and the mother ran towards her. The labourer felt at ease and calmed the mother who remained still. He went for her with an attitude expressing: "nothing has happened." He carefully took the little muzzle out and did not put it on again until the following week. When a mistake occurs during training, this is not fixed unless it is immediately repeated because there is not enough time to place it in the long-term memory.

What happens when a horse has a traffic accident or when it is attacked or ill-treated by a person or an animal? Due to the fact that these experiences significantly affect its life because it is terribly scared and in pain, it immediately fixes those experiences in its memory. The horse can overcome negative memories if we work with patience and with the intention of rebuilding its confidence. However, it is necessary to bear in mind that the old reaction might reappear if the animal is exposed to great tension or to a similar risky situation.

CHAPTER IV

LEARNING

Bathing the Red Horse (Petrov-Vodkin – 1912)

WHAT DOES LEARNING MEAN FOR A SOCIAL ANIMAL?

Previously, we discussed the areas of the brain in which learning takes place. Let us see now how this process is developed. A social animal like the horse needs to know who it is as soon as it is born. That is, it needs to understand its identity as a horse: that it is a prey animal and that, faced with danger; it has to flee quickly as a survival response. The learning process has a specific function: the animal needs to be able to live, survive and preserve itself as a species.

Learning, apprenticeship, information, communication, transmission. What do these words mean? We need more comprehensive meanings for the purpose of this study.

Learning: To acquire knowledge about something through study or experience. Get something into the memory.

Apprenticeship: (from apprentice) Act and result of learning a given art, job or something else. The time devoted to it. In psychology: acquisition through continuous practice.

Inform: Literally, it means to give form. Nowadays, the word refers to the origin of the form or the order in the world. Information refers to the informative, and it functions as a training cause, as for example the concept of "genetic information." Notify, break the news of something. Give substantial form to something. Shape, improve someone through instruction and proper upbringing.

Communicate: Participate with other people in what we have. Discover, express or inform someone of something. Talk, deal verbally with someone. Transmit signals by means of a code common both for speaker and recipient.

Communication: Act and result of communicating something or communicating between people. Treatment, correspondence between two or more people.

With these definitions in mind, it is possible to conceptualise the horses' learning process as a set of responses triggered by the teacher (who, in turn, also learns) and produced through an information and communication process by means of which information is incorporated and responses are elaborated; a dynamical, bilateral process, in which both parties learn from information and energy exchange.

Chapter IV

It is worth mentioning that there is a species behaviour and individual behaviour. Species behaviour is based on instinctive responses, but the way in which these are expressed varies with each animal; therefore, as for individual conduct, each animal behaves differently according to personality, heredity, breeding and circumstances.

Since it is difficult to differentiate between instinctive and learned conducts, Lucy Rees, a Welsh expert in ethology and natural taming of horses, helps us with the following example: "According to some scientists, the study of some birds' complex singing, with no apparent practice, can only be carried out through careful manipulation of the birds' environment during the first moments of life, in order to know whether they are born with the ability to sing in a specific tone, or if they reach that tone through trial and error, or if they imitate other birds' singing. However, the difference between learned and instinctive behaviour can be easily seen in our domestic animals."

Trainers take advantage of the different abilities horses have in order to prepare them for different disciplines.

WHAT IS A GENETIC PROGRAM?

A genetic program is a predetermined procedure or plan every organism inherits with their genes. According to some scientists, domestication is the process by which a species adapts to men and to captivity situations; in this process, certain epigenetic changes and adaptation processes occur, brought about by the environment and the surrounding circumstances, and which recur through generations. Adaptation ability is an aptitude horses have, and it is aimed at preserving the species. This adaptation process is evolutionary and gradual; it occurs during long periods of time and involves the genetic fixation of morphological, physiological and behavioural adaptations.

Heredity is the transfer of characteristics from ancestors to descendants. Originally, it was understood in a broad sense, including the heredity of characteristics and vital habits; but mechanistic biology restricted its use only to the inheritance of genes. According to Harvard biochemist Rupert Sheldrake's hypothesis of the formative cause, heredity includes both genetic heredity and heredity of morphogenetic fields, which carry characteristics and vital habits that are transmitted in time.

The first men who selected horses chose the strongest, fastest and most docile ones. Those first horses did not know how to behave with men and had to be tamed – trained. Training causes behaviour changes in animals, changes that depend on the characteristics of the experience reinforcement in the environment and with people, and which are shown as permanent behaviour changes in horses. This is the difference between learned behaviour and genetically determined behaviour.

Learned behaviour causes a lasting change because the experience is recorded and accumulated in the long-term memory, and produces physical changes in the neuronal organisation. But it can be altered if the characteristics of environmental reinforcement change.

WHAT IS TRAINING?

"Training" is a word usually used to refer to the act of teaching something to an animal. "Training" means: to prepare, to coach people or animals, especially for sports. The word "teach", also used in connection with animals, comes from "teacher", from teaching or coaching; taming an animal, sometimes teaching him different skills.

In order to coach or train animals, the trainer simultaneously uses the positive external reinforcements and the animals' inner motivation to please others and to do their work correctly.

You can stimulate horses with your voice, saying: "let's go" and stop them with an "oooooh." Work is usually carried out with the intention of creating a connection based on mutual feelings of fondness between rider and horse although unfortunately, some people do not care about horses and only use them, dominate them or treat them violently; like the rodeo rider who was thrown by his horse, whom he had evidently subjugated, and when he was interviewed by a TV channel he answered brutally, "Now to the pasture to fatten him up and send him to the cold storage plant."

Well-treated horses are very fond of people who ride, train or take care of them. When there is a harmonic relationship, certain indispensable cravings in wild life diminish, because animals that are well treated and cared for, "free themselves from instincts" and are "available" to learn at different levels. It is as if the brain, not having to pay attention to survival, acquires abilities, in its sensitive area, to "learn" more refined conditionings, such as the ones triggered during the taming process. In his book *Man Meets Dog*, Konrad Lorenz says that, in their relationship with men, horses have lost some of their ancestors' instincts, but they have gained communication and expression abilities. Many animals have proved they are able to develop new abilities thanks to a beneficial contact with men.

DIFFERENT WAYS OF LEARNING

In order to respond precisely and efficiently, animals *learn to learn*. And each animal has his own time and way of learning.

Chapter IV

Non-associative learning or habituation

A habit is a way of doing something, a custom, a mental or physical condition which occurs in a specific way and which is acquired by frequent repetition.

Horses learn to sharpen their fleeing reaction according to the degree of real danger; thus they are gifted with a great ability for distinguishing what is dangerous and what is not. Apart from this, they have a great capacity of habituation to adapt to the different noises of the environment in wild life. Trainers, knowingly or not, use this capacity to vaccinate them, shoe them, mount them, or make them walk in roads filled with cars. During training, horses get used to these actions and get desensitised, to not react to stimulus that would normally cause fear. Therefore, *habituation is the decrease or disappearance of a certain response to repeated stimuli,* which is not caused by any process of association. For example, a foal can get accustomed to the noise or the gleam of a plastic bag. The first time it sees it, it may get scared; but if the trainer shows it to the foal from different angles, making noises and bringing it closer or moving it away, always staying calm, the foal finally stops showing fear because it gets used to the plastic bag stimulus, since it understands it does not hurt. When it realises it is not in danger, it overcomes the instinctive responses of escape, distance or fight. Racing or jumping horses who live in city clubs, get used to walking in the middle of the traffic, ignoring the noises of the cars passing near them.

It is a temporal, gradual learning, since horses who are stressed or under a lot of pressure may forget what they have learnt, or will react with fear before the slightest change in the situation, so slight that it is often imperceptible for those near them. This phenomenon is called *dishabituation* because, given the appearance of slightly different stimuli from those used during the habituation process, the response reappears (that is, loss of the acquired habit). For example, a horse that is used to a certain road may get scared at the sudden appearance of a shiny plastic bag or a huge metal container. In order to make them familiar with the environment and its context, some trainers take young horses to the places where they will compete: racetracks, jumping clubs, polo matches and endurance tests.

To familiarise means to get someone in touch with the new situations in which he will live. A new horse, used to the place where it usually lives, may get scared the first time it goes out to compete; but if it gets familiarised or accustomed to the different situations it will encounter, it will get used to them, and will surely follow the rider as it does at "home."

Horses' minds work in an integrated, holistic and gestaltic manner, that is, they grasp the entire situation in which they are in. Due to this ability, a horse accustomed to getting on trailers, for example, may get scared one day due to some kind of subtle stimulus people do not perceive, but which it does, and refuse to get on it because it believes it might be dangerous. Maybe the horse smells an unfamiliar smell, or perceives the presence of a dog at a certain distance, some kind of change in the entire situation. Some people who are unaware of this type of behaviour do not take the time to see what may have changed and blame the horse for its attitude, as if the poor animal were doing it on purpose. They expect to solve the difficulty by punishing it with violence, as can be seen at some racetracks or jumping clubs. This attitude only makes matters worse, since the horse gets terrified. During the transfer of some horses, one of them was very scared and refused to budge, it did not move. First, they brought a horse who was a friend of it and then the driver took the truck to a place where they made a protection on both sides of the ramp and made it get up backwards. Apparently, the horse had once hit its head and therefore refused to get in. The solution was to offer it security, trying to make it understand that nothing "bad" was going to happen, and so the horse understood, got on the trailer and travelled well.

The vision of the horse is panoramic. Its first feeling when getting into a trailer is to enter into a space where it cannot escape. Therefore, if you get it used to entering a box when it is a foal, it is possible to accustom it to get on the trailer, as long as you do it with care and patience.

It is advisable to make it used to as many situations that it may have to face in the future as possible, so that it can completely fix them in the mind. For example, if you want to teach it to cross a bridge, you should make it go through several similar situations, which will make it feel a certain unsteadiness, such as making it walk over cloth or plastics, materials that will make it uneasy.

In very much the same way as with the previous example, it is all about the animal getting used to the different stimuli so that when it has to cross a bridge, it already knows something about that situation. The essential thing in this case is the unsteadiness it feels, the ground's texture, or the lack of security on both sides.

In order to make learning efficient, it must be frequently repeated. The habituation process is more effective if you work in short periods of exposure to the stimulus, especially if the horse is young or new.

In brief: habituation or non-associative learning is the simplest way of learning, and it brings about a behavioural change induced by experience.

Learning by conditioning or association

Conditioning or association is the creation of a bond between a stimulus and a response, a conditioning which is activated by reinforcement. Reinforcement can be positive or negative, depending on what needs to be taught. There are two types of conditionings.

Chapter IV

Classical or Pavlovian conditioning (Type I)

There is a behavioural change that depends on what happens in two situations. Immediately after a stimulus, a reinforcement is produced and the mind associates these situations. The animal shows a behaviour related to the reinforcement to which it was exposed. An investigator called Pavlov carried out a series of experiments with dogs. Dogs salivated when he walked into the room and he thought this was due to the fact that they associated his entrance with food, but then he observed that a light or a bell could also cause salivation if dogs were fed at the same time a light was switched on or a bell rang. He started by showing meat to the dogs, at the same time as he rang a bell; after repeating this action several times, dogs salivated only by hearing the bell.

A *positive reinforcement* is something pleasant, like the food that the dogs from Pavlov's experience got after hearing a bell. A *negative reinforcement* is something unpleasant, like the electric shock horses get when they touch an electric fence.

This type of conditioning is used for training almost all animals. Association is produced when reinforcement is simultaneous to or immediately follows the response, and through repetition of the situation, so that it can be fixed in the long-term memory.

Some horses feel bad or get scared or excited when they see the blacksmith or the veterinarian, because it associates them with negative experiences, such as one horse who got terrified when it saw a syringe, because it had been conditioned that the syringe caused it pain. Before doing something unpleasant, it is useful to stroke or talk to them, to take some time to be in close contact with them, so that animals remember something pleasant before and after the unpleasant action. Sometimes, stroking or talking to them is enough to build trust. Many veterinarians and blacksmiths do so, and horses respond well to this treatment. Sometimes, when horses are very frightened, it is even advisable to let them loose for a while, without putting too much pressure on them, so that they can relax and the manoeuvre is much easier. When horses feel they can flee, and you do not put too much pressure on them, they calm down. Then it is possible to manoeuvre them calmly.

Thanks to this conditioning, they learn some information that allows them to predict the future, and so they behave accordingly, such as when "feeding" time comes. Either in a club or with loose horses in paddocks, when they are about to be fed they get anxious because they learned to associate all the data meaning: "I'm going to be fed." In their mind, they associate the time, the circumstances, the smells and the movements of the person in charge of feeding them. Many managers of fields, use buckets filled with oats, and make some noise with them so as to attract the horses who are loose and far away. In some cases, if the person in charge of feeding them takes more time to get there, some horses call him by neighing, or get restless and walk near the gate, waiting for him.

Human behaviour, as well as animal behaviour, is fundamentally based on this type of associative conditioning, including tastes and aversions, habits, concerns and motivations.

Due to the associative conditioning, the animal adjusts it's behaviour in order to receive rewards and to avoid negative things, depending on the reinforcement received.

The animal will then start looking for those situations that give it pleasure and will try to avoid those that hurt it.

Instrumental operative by trial and error conditioning (Type II)

In this type of conditioning, there is a link between a stimulus and a voluntary answer from the animal, as a result of a given reinforcement. It is the typical trial and error learning, such as the newly born foal that has to improve its suckling skills. This learning, through trial and error, is common to all mammals. It entails the repetition of an action that causes pleasure and the avoidance of an action that may cause discomfort.

Another typical example is the horse that sticks his head out of the box when its owner arrives, and gives it carrots to eat. Thus, it learns quickly and by chance, that when the owner comes and it sticks its head out of the box, it gets carrots. The horse associates the action of receiving carrots – reward or reinforcement – with its casual behaviour.

Much training is based on this method, basically because the animal "wants" to behave in a certain way since it gets a reward. Some trainers motivate animals with food. They give them a sign, like a specific sound, so that they perform the expected behaviour and, simultaneously or immediately after, they give them food. Food is the reward or positive reinforcement; the lack of it is the negative reinforcement.

Since we work with the horses' will, it is advisable to stimulate them without making them suffer. Therefore, we motivate and reward them so that they enjoy performing their tasks. When you work with a new horse, it may not understand what you tell it and react in an undesired way. In such cases, it is better to ignore this reaction until it understands and learns through positive conditioning, without any punishment.

Reinforcement is positive if the answer is rewarded, and negative if the answer is unrewarded. That is, through positive reinforcement, the animal is encouraged to make a certain movement and, when it does, it is congratulated.

For example, when it is taught to follow the one who leads him by a halter, as soon as it intends to follow the person, the pressure is released by loosening the halter.

Through negative reinforcement, it is encouraged not to do certain things, giving it a pleasant moment when it stops doing them. For example, when a horse retreats its steps, the halter is shaken; and when it stops, it is released from the pressure caused by the shaking of the halter.

In order to eliminate a negative conditioning, the association between response and reinforcement needs to be deconstructed, for example, stop giving it carrots when the horse sticks its head out of the box. This is an adequate practice for horses who are prone to biting, as they have been conditioned and reinforced through the delivery of food, and have become biters, especially stallions.

Learning through association is a biological phenomenon both for human beings and animals. Some of the factors that influence learning are: circumstances, heredity, personality and memory. A certain part of memory may be genetic and will probably allow horses who were trained in a particular discipline to transmit that "knowledge" to their descendants. That is why breeders "sell" genes.

Some mechanistic researchers believe that even conditioned voluntary responses are not be under any form of conscious control and that horses act mechanically. If so, why do they sometimes make the connection between stimulus and response and sometimes they do not? Are they machines that fail or that do not understand? Many times, they do not understand what they are asked to do and, contrary to a machine, they have feelings, states of mind and emotions that make them behave in a different way each day, states that influence their learning and attention abilities and, in turn, the decisions they make.

Horses learn to associate all the stimuli they receive from the rider: voice, signals they perceive through the reins, legs, weight and balance. In different places around the world, it is usual to say: "oooh" to ask the horse to stop or slow the pace, together with a sign from the rider if he is mounting the horse, or with a sign from the rein if he is in a round pen.

In time, horses learn to stop or slow down when they hear the "oooh." Once they associate the stimulus with the action, the same reaction will take place, which means that it is transformed into a habit that becomes stronger and difficult to change, be it good or bad. Horses that learn very complex actions, are rewarded at the beginning when they try to perform the exercise; but as they learn more complex exercises, they get rewards only when the effort is bigger. As they learn, they elaborate even more complex and subtle responses. When training is more advanced, there is a complex combination of conditioned and non-conditioned stimuli.

Imprinting or engraving

A. K. Lorenz, Austrian ethologist, conducted an experiment of separating some goose eggs from the mother. He observed during hatching that, when the goslings saw him, instead of an escape reaction, they adopted the innate instinctive behaviour of

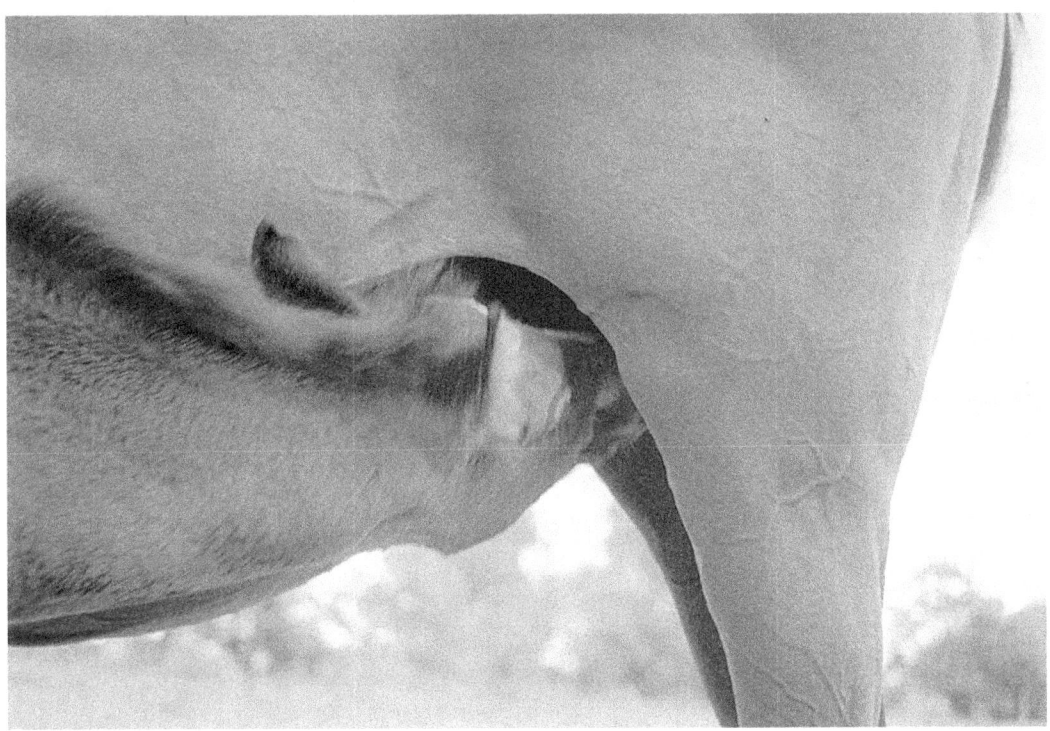

Picture 24: Every instinctive act is performed in a particular way which depends on the horse's intelligence.

Picture 25: A well trained horse learns to understand his rider even without the bit.

Pictures 26 and 27: Social learning. The foal learns from his mother and by observing the rest of the herd.

Picture 28: Foals tend to follow their mothers' behavior.

Picture 29: Frutillito. Early stimulation.

Pictures 30 and 31: Horses learn to be horses within their group.

following the first thing they found, in this case, a human being. He also observed that they could follow another animal or even an object. Lorenz named this process imprinting or engraving.

The animal who accepts the person as if it were his "mother" in her absence has difficulties to accept one of his own species because he "engraves or imprints" the person. Apparently, higher animals are supposed to have a more developed capacity of engraving than lower animals. When higher birds and mammals are born, they have certain latency in relation to determined schemes, a latency that might be called "disposition to engrave", which means that the offspring of these animals are born with certain complete schemes in relation to the environment.

Shortly after birth some animals, especially prey animals, experience a process by which the newly born receives the information from the mother about what it is and what it will be during its life. This means that the foal finds out that it is a prey animal and that it will become a horse and will have to pay attention to certain situations that will be dangerous.

It is a non-intentional learning process that does not depend on the repetition of associations and it is characterised by a fast and early learning process in mammals and birds, during which the species behaviour patterns are established. The imprint is related to maternity or food. Although it is a lasting impression, it was thought to be irreversible, contrary to other forms of learning, and when a young animal was always near its mother, it would be incapable of learning that something or someone else could be its mother. In the case of foals, the idea is related to following a big object that moves or learning where they can suckle or try to suckle. If there is no reinforcement (milk, in this case), this big object that moves will be rejected. Therefore, it is reversible, and foals that were always near their mothers might learn to suckle from other mothers if theirs happen to die. For this reason, it is possible to feed an orphan foal if it is starving, because it can learn to drink from a bottle. As in the case of a foal that lost its mother and was adopted by an old mare, its mother's friend. Although she did not have milk, she did the breastfeeding ritual, aided by the workers of the place who gave the bottle to the foal.

Nature seems to programme the newly born so that they can quickly identify their mother, their protector. The newly born needs to trust it´s mother and to learn from it.

Dr. Miller, (U.S.A), who has worked with foals for years, observed that when he examined a foal several months after birth, this foal recognised him, even after such a long time. When he went to see the foal for a second time, the horse behaved calmly, he was easy to handle and there where no dangerous situations for the doctor or the foal. As Miller was familiar with Lorenz's experience, he developed an imprinting system with newly born foals, that implies interacting with the horse within the first half hour

Chapter IV

after birth. He recommends doing this for two consecutive days because those are the days when they learn fastest. This process of learning after birth is called "early learning."

In some way, when we make this imprint we tell the foal that we are as reliable as its mother. You work with the mother beside the foal, allowing eye contact to avoid breaking the bond between them. It is a delicate technique that consists of a series of manoeuvers and movements with the foal. The aim is to get it accustomed to certain manoeuvers it will experience as an adult, such as hand contact in different parts of its body, which are softly done for a brief period of time until the foal accepts them. It is recommended to work for short periods of time to avoid boredom or saturation.

I have obtained very good results working this way for about 10 or 15 minutes a day, over 3 or 4 consecutive days, beginning just a few days after birth. I believe that during the first days, the foal needs to be with its mother. During this process, it is useful for it to get accustomed to our voice, to become familiar with our smell, our movement and everything related to us.

Indians, who lived with horses were familiar with this practice with foals because horses were like brothers to them. On many occasions, that brotherhood marked the difference between living and dying, so they had a more intimate relationship with their animals. The enemy admired that connection they could not have with their own horses. From when they were born, foals were accustomed to being touched – as we say in my country, Argentina, "descosquillados"[1] – to voices and to other types of manoeuvers. Even when they were educated, Indians taught them to gallop with *boleadoras*[2] by their hooves, or to wait for the enemy by lying down, hidden in the bushes so as to take them by surprise. The enemy army that did not respect them and, unfortunately, devastated them.

Indians had a similar relationship with wild horses. They were simple, patient and compassionate with their quadruped friends. Descendents of the Mapuche aborigines say: "When they had nothing left to eat, and their horse was the only thing they had, before killing him, they apologised, said a prayer of gratitude, and avoided cruelty"... This is quite a lesson!

Imprinting is a simple but, at the same time, delicate method, in which the most important thing is to listen to the foal and be very patient, delicate and have common sense because otherwise there will be serious consequences. Techniques always depend upon the person who makes use of them.

This technique is beneficial because, as horses have confidence in men, they understand when they need to pay attention and voluntarily collaborate. In general, they arrive calmly at the dressage, are easy to handle, get on the trailer tamely and let people examine them.

---

1   To remove the sensation of being tickled. To desensitise.
2   Leather thongs tipped with leather-covered stones

At a stud farm, the owner's daughter "desensitised" her Hackney crossbred filly. The way she concentrated during the course was so impressive that participants were surprised at the difference with other horses. Another crossbred horse, that was used during the "jineteada"[3], was attentive, noble and focused on its work; however, it was quite serious. Although it was trying to trust people, it was evident that it held some memory that prevented it from gaining confidence. On the other hand, the filly was relaxed, attentive but mainly confident.

Some breeders use different situations to stimulate their foals, and so to get them accustomed to their future lives. They put halters on them, blankets over their backs to prepare them for the saddle, raise their hooves and legs, and do other exercises such as putting on the muzzle and removing it, touching their ears, opening their mouth, or taking them to the chute behind their mothers so they learn to stay calm at the place and, if they can, they get them into the trailer with their mothers. These types of manoeuvers produce confident adult horses, save money and time and, basically, decreases the risk of losing horses.

If teaching methods are efficiently applied and foals retain the experience as beneficial, the result will also be beneficial. Positive intention – positive energy – positive result. Apparently, early experiences have an "imprint" effect, as when a wild foal learns to run in irregular terrain as soon as it is born. If it succeeds, it will obviously be more apt to do it throughout the rest of its life.

The first days of life are the best ones to incorporate experiences that will remain strongly imprinted. Foals that live alone during the first months of life cannot learn the normal socialisation codes. They are like orphans who spend time solely near humans, and believe they are their peers and treat them accordingly.

The equine code should be quickly transmitted to orphan foals, so they learn not to invade personal space, something that frequently happens. If they do not learn these limits, they become spoiled and, when they come into contact with adult horses, they run the risk of being kicked and hurt.

The most important thing to diminish fear of men is the handling frequency. The foal needs to be familiarised with people. Some breeders recommend their employees wander around the pastures where there are a lot of mares who have just foaled, so the newly born get accustomed to people. According to their experiences, it is useful in the relationship they establish. On the contrary, when people get close to them in a rude or unconscious way, they teach them to fear. A well treated foal "naturally" learns to work pretty well with men because it does what it would naturally do with its mother.

---

3   Breaking in horses

Chapter IV

Learning through observation or social learning (imitative or by emulation)

This learning is produced by observing others' behaviour and by the social need for belonging. Basically, it allows the animal to feel that it belongs to the group and it is also a way of learning standards of behaviour. It is easy to observe the way foals tend to follow their mother's behaviour. If she is a friend of so-and-so, her offspring will also be a friend and, accordingly, they reject those that the mother rejects, or respect those their mother respects. If the mother approaches someone, they do it; if the mother wards off flies, they do it and even in a similar way. In an establishment there was a mare who had just foaled, who became friends with a training horse who came to rest; the foal considered it a referent and sometimes it even moved away from its mother and ate at the other horse's side. Animals observe others' behaviour in detail and try to do the same. They can also imitate people's actions, such as the mare who learned to open a gate by moving the plank they had used to lock it.

She observed, from a distance, when they locked the gate and a few hours later, she went there and unlocked it. Once you follow a model, there is a "permanent" change of conduct.

This is produced in stages:

- Acquisition: the learner observes a model and recognises the distinctive features of its behaviour.
- Retention: responses of the model are actively stored in the memory.
- Execution: the learner accepts the model's behaviour as appropriate because it gets benefits from it and thus reproduces it.
- Consequences: if the behaviour brings benefits, it is strengthened; on the contrary, if it brings negative consequences, it is weakened by a process of operative conditioning.

This learning is common among social animals (even among children and adults) who, in order to keep themselves alive, need basic information about the environment, food and water sources, and dangers; information that is acquired from the actions of their relatives. It is useful because it is a reliable way of learning about the world. It requires a degree of conscience and attention to what other people do and also to the consequences of their actions. It is a fast learning process with less risks than trial and error.

Dr. Marthe Kiley-Worthington, an English expert in equine behaviour, has observed that her students – horses, dogs, cows and llamas – were able to imitate their human teachers in the performance of very simple movements. They used this technique to teach and it worked so well that now they perform an "imitation dance" in which every animal emulates their teacher's movements at the sound of music. Imitation tells us something about animals' levels of conscious awareness. That is the reason why this is something that should be taken into account when teaching strategies are designed.

Horses learn to be horses within their group. Logically, this learning method is used, for example, when a horse goes into the trailer for the first time. If a new or shy horse sees another one doing it, it will feel more motivated to do it; on the contrary, if he sees another horse that does not want to go into the trailer, he will be scared and will refuse to do it.

In general, mares who trust men have self-confident foals. Foals learn from their mothers how to behave with humans. Observing her mother, a filly learns how to place herself for getting massages. It is funny because each of them places themselves at one side of the masseuse who looks like a sandwich between the two.

Silent or exploratory learning (latent)

This is produced by the acquisition of information from the world that surrounds us, frequently without even noticing that it is happening, in an almost constant way. Behaviour is modified without any apparent reason. It is not instantly manifested but it is adopted by subsequent behaviour that is "awakened" by some eventuality. Thorpe defines it as the association of unrewarded, latent stimuli.

Animals are good at exploring their territory and taking as much information as possible, which will be later used for different situations that may arise, different eventualities. It is a way of learning that remains latent and does not depend on rewards or constant repetition. It is vital for wild animals that use it to find their way in their territory. The essential part of this process is animals' exploration ability. It is similar to associative learning but it does not imply a reward. An example of this exploration and memory ability is that of horses that were sold and, months later, returned "home." Some data remains unconsciously stored in the long-term memory and, although the animal does not need to use it immediately, data is at its disposal to be used at the necessary moment. It is an ability to "anticipate."

To register information from the environment implies that they might remember tracks and recognise objects even if they are out of place.

A dog called "Chicho" that apparently did not look smart while living with its previous owners, was taken in by an acquaintance when they moved. The dog barked a lot and was distrustful. The new owner tried to take it to his place, but could not. The dog stayed in the street for a month or so. Near his old house, there was an intersection of three avenues with three traffic lights.

Chapter IV

Chicho crossed perfectly well at all corners. It knew when it had to go from one street to the other. I believe this is a good example of silent observation learning. It had probably learnt to follow people, but it had also learned silently every other waiting factor: now this way, now this other way, now you have to wait, what we actually do when we are at a road with so many crossings.

Discernment (insight) or problem solving

This is the highest way of learning and is related to reasoning. This type of learning has been proved in some animals that solve problems fast. In humans, it is also called intuitive learning.

My mare was able to discern in the following situation: during summer, which was extremely dry that year, she learned that when she drank water, she could throw it into the soil and make a quagmire where she could roll over and refresh herself. How can we take this fact objectively? There were more than thirty horses at this field and no one did this. She was a racing mare and, according to some research, racing horses have some atavistic genes, by the mere fact of running. She used to spend a great amount of time near the huge blue water container and she never saw a horse making mud. So she gathered certain data in her mind and, when she recognised it, she acted effectively to take a bath and refresh herself. One day they were covering the pit she had made and she stayed by the workers' side, staring at them as if to say: "what are you doing with my pit?"

This process implies reasoning; it is a process in which two or more isolated experiences are spontaneously combined to form a new and effective experience to achieve a goal. Discernment, or deep knowledge, might be defined like the immediate comprehension and adequate response to a new situation without trial and error being necessary.

Horses are not prepared for reasoning because their minds have evolved and adapted in response to their immediate needs and to the pressure of the environment.

Their priority is survival; therefore, they act in the first place. Even though they do not need to analyse situations, they store in their memories what they have learnt. By means of this process of learning, animals arrive at a conclusion without trial and error, as if they had recognised how to solve the situation. According to some researchers, this "realising" is a latent learning that arises from games or other early experiences.

Different types of learning

• Non-associative learning or habituation
• Learning by conditioning or association Classical or Pavlovian conditioning (type I) Operative, instrumental or trial and error conditioning (type II)
• Imprinting or engraving
• Learning through observation or social learning (imitative or by emulation)
• Silent or exploratory learning (latent)
• Discernment (insight) or problem solving

CHAPTER V

TEACHING AND GAMES

The Circus (Granville – 19th C)

It was a strip of fire
Galloping, galloping.
Mane tousled in blazes.
My Alazan, it's you I'm naming.
                Atahualpa Yupanqui

GNOMO

I open this chapter with the story of a horse I had to train when I was a little girl. This experience was most enriching for me since I learnt a lot, and it encouraged me to study horses' behaviour, their communication system and different teaching methods that did not resort to ill-treatment, violence or harshness.

When I was sixteen I lived in a neighbourhood that was near a riding club we had opened. A relative of mine had a beautiful racing horse, a crossbreed between Criollo and Purebred. It was a sorrel foal, with a white stripe; his name was Gnomo. The name described him accurately because he was one of the most cheerful and naughtiest animals I had ever met. He was starting to work when he tore a muscle on his right superficial thigh, which kept him in rest for a long time. Since they could not pay a lot of attention to the foal they asked me if I could take care of him, and I accepted since I was really interested in the foal. I learnt patience and realised that you can teach by playing, because I literally played with him and, in this way, he learnt everything I could intuitively teach him. He would give me his hooves, and would come running to meet me when I got to the club. He understood what I told him, perhaps because I spoke to him a lot and at the same time I suggested certain exercises. This was really a great horse for me.

The first times I mounted him, he threw me two or three times, because he was very strong, full of energy, with eagerness and a need to let his nature flow. I could understand what he needed and I started working with him tied to a rope.

I spoke a lot to him and had a lot of fun with him. As time went by, he got used to being with me and when I mounted him, even if he was full of energy, I talked to him and said: "It's O.K. Gnomo, you can play but don't throw me." The foal understood, since he only bucked slightly but with no intention of throwing me. He never threw me again. I let him loose as much as I could, and when I got to the club and approached

Chapter V

the gate, I whistled to him and called his name, and he would come running to meet me, neighing with joy, and stand on his back hooves to greet me. He also did this when he worked at the pen and I told him: "It's O.K. Gnomo, I love it when you greet me, but be careful because you can hurt me." He never touched me with his equine greetings. Other times, when I got there he would be inside his box, which was at the other side of the entrance. I would let him know I was coming, calling him or making jokes, and he started knocking at the door. One day, I played too many jokes on him, so that he grabbed my thumb with his mouth – I still have the mark – and at that moment I realised I had made him overexcited, so I told him "You are right, please let go my thumb ", and so he did. Otherwise, today I would have a thumb missing.

Although I had a riding teacher, I did not have anyone who taught me how to train a horse. Gnomo had to be re-educated because he had been locked inside his box for six months. I used my common sense; I worked with him every day, patiently and with a lot of dedication. I really loved working with him, since he was, apart from naughty and mischievous, very intelligent. He understood everything I asked him to do. There was empathy between us from the beginning, despite the falls. Ten months after beginning to work with him, there was an internal competition at my club and I had the opportunity of making his debut. As usually happens at clubs, some managers did not know much about horses and said that Gnomo was a "crazy" and "useless" horse. On the day of his first competition, I spent a lot of time walking him around the track, for almost half an hour, while I spoke to him and told him : "Today we need to be perfect", "We are going to show them how good we are"; I both stimulated myself and my little horse. When we walked onto the track, he started bucking but – and this was really impressive – once we started walking, he was impeccable.

We jumped along a one-meter terrain and we broke the tie with the best horses of the club, those that jumped in higher levels and we won the competition! beating the best horses, even Malenky my dapple grey horse, who was very efficient. It was a great achievement.

I remember Gnomo understood my moods; our communication was subtle. Such was the case when one day we were working around some trees at the front of the club, facing a road. Between the road and the club there was a path where people who ran horse races and some trotters practiced. That day, while we were working through trees, a pervert stood opposite me and opened his pants. So, without thinking, I told the horse "Let's go Gnomo!" We left at a gallop, jumped the fence and when we approached the man, Gnomo stood on his hooves and attacked him!!! I had never taught him to stand on his feet!!! Evidently, he understood he had to defend me. The guy apologised and started running and we followed him.

I really taught that horse from inside myself. I did it intuitively and we had a lot of fun. For example, on Fridays I used to take him to run along the race track. It was the day when I would let him completely loose and how he ran! He was like the wind. I could not get mad at him, because I realised that if he did not do something, it was because he did not understand. At the end of the club there was a slope that filled with water and mud during rainy times. So I made him walk there. Those were our adventures. And every time he worked hard, I took him for a ride so that he could rest.

Unfortunately, one day he was sold and I was heartbroken. A year later, I saw him at his new the club. When I got there I called him, without knowing where he was, and he neighed at me, and when I got to his box this vivacious horse laid his head on my shoulder and stood still. I mounted him that day and I could not believe what they had done to him. He was tight and tense; he was another horse. He was not my Gnomo. Sadly, these are some of the stories that we have to experience. I stood behind him and he relaxed his leg so that I could clean his hoof. The person who had bought him also used to ask him for the hoof but he did not give it to him. Gnomo never liked this guy.

That is an example of how noble and loyal horses are. Even today, I miss Gnomo. I know that he finally went to a gaucho who was proud of the things he did with the horse. He would have been a great jumping horse in his category. I had the opportunity of giving him his debut at an external competition for new horses and he also gave a great performance. We finished in fourth place due to a knock down we had because I was going too fast.

TEACHING – TRAINING

In our *Martin Fierro* we find these verses which, with great clarity and precision, express the teaching method used by the people who had a good relationship with their horses, either Indians or gauchos.

> *And so, anyone whose aim it is*
> *to own a model horse*
> *has to care for it tirelessly,*
> *and he's also got to see*
> *that no one uses the whip on it*
> *or drag at its mouth when it's down.*

Chapter V

I was also like that crazy man
(Molina Campos, 1959)

Many people think they'll break a horse
by cruelty and the whip
and if they see it's an ugly-looking beast
that shows signs of viciousness,
they'll lash its head tight to a stake
till it pulls its neck out of joint.

A man who understands these things
has an advantage over the rest.
It's good to learn because there are few
horse-tamers worth the name,
and a lot of bunglers going round
with a tamer's halter and rein.

They'll use all sorts of excuses
and ways to get round saddling it:
they say it's to break the horse's will
but any fool can tell
it's because they're afraid of how it'll buck
and they won't admit to it.

The horse is an animal
excuse me for mentioning it -
which has plenty of good sense
and plenty of feelings too:
it's a creature that thrives on affection,
and it's patience that conquers it.

JOSÉ HERNÁNDEZ

In his book *The Art of Horsemanship*, Xenophon (Greece, 5th C BC), a cavalry soldier and horse riding expert, left us a legacy of knowledge about how to educate horses. It is remarkable that the way of treating horses still has a similarity with the type of treatment many ancient cultures employed and, even today, as some Bedouin and Turkmen tribes do.

Even though this is not a book about training, it is useful to remember some rules for educating horses.

What is the aim of teaching?

The aim of teaching is to put the potential into action. The verb "to teach" has many meanings, for example: instruct, train with rules and precepts, set an example or teach a lesson that serves as an experience for future situations. To indicate, give signals of something. Get used to, habituate to something.

Teaching is a system and method for giving instructions. It is the set of knowledge, principles and ideas that are transmitted to someone. "Teaching" and "teach" are broad terms, which can be used with great precision. A useful referent for focusing on this aspect of the relationship with horses is: *interaction*

Sarcophagus of a Sidonia ruler
(Greek Art – 330 BC)

within the process of information exchange, even when dealing with horses, because it can be considered a mutual enrichment process, since it is an opportunity of learning about horses and about us. Horses are great mirrors of the people they establish a relationship with. Both turn into subjects of the world, who get enriched and become aware of each other, if the one who teaches focuses the training on this kind of reference, instead of focusing on the outdated and inefficient, authoritarian and violent ones.

It is possible to focus so as to establish a connection with the horse and understand where his mind is, in order to establish a relationship of mutual respect in which the horse sharply *communicates* with his body and mind.

When do handling problems appear?

Problems occur during learning, when a horse receives positive reinforcements that he should not receive. Unfortunately this happens very often, due to lack of knowledge. Some owners positively reinforce their horses by, for example, giving them food when they bite the box's door.

Chapter V

Even though their intention is to calm them down, they only get them to bite the door even more, in order to get food.

Another example is the situation in which the horse has to do something for the first time – such as taking part in an endurance test – without any kind of preparation, without having been accustomed to similar situations so that the first experience is calm and non-traumatic. In these cases, it is useful to resort to silent learning. Some people who have vehicles take their new horses for a "ride"; this is a positive experience which makes the horse calm when getting into the vehicle the day he has to run or jump.

In short, handling problems appear when you do not pay attention to the horses' way of communication. And especially when you positively reinforce them when you should not, or when you do not reward them when you should. It is worth mentioning that between these two situations, there are many variations.

What happens with punishment?

Punishment usually only causes fear. A horse that experiences fear cannot learn and will ultimately associate the entire situation with fear and punishment. On the other hand, reward works the same as with children; when they do something right, they are congratulated and this encourages them to do it better every time, since rewards facilitate the process.

In Spain, I worked with a Purebred Spanish stallion. A beautiful, huge animal with dapple hair. When I approached him and made eye contact, I asked myself: "What have they done to him ?" He looked at me as if saying: "What are you going to do to me?" such was the fear he transmitted. According to the person who took care of him, the problem he had was that, when they tried to put him inside the coach, he would lay down on the ground. I tried to make him run but he did not dare. I continued asking because there was something I did not understand and, finally, the truth came out. What did they do when he sat down? They beat him! I had to explain to this person – a professional – that he sat down because he was scared, although we did not know why.

But by beating him, they only frightened him even more and blocked him. I guess he must have fallen down some day and could not get up or got caught, or every time they tied him up to the coach they beat him. I took him to a chute to see how he reacted. I had the intention of recreating in his memory a similar situation to being caught on both sides. The result was that he came in and out without difficulties. We went backwards and forwards, I let him do what he pleased. I wanted him to feel he could leave whenever he wanted and that if he stayed, he did it out of his own will. He turned out fine. I suggested the owners do the same on the coach, to let him loose so that he would not feel too much pressure, and to reward him by letting him out so that, through those positive actions, he could understand that nothing would happen to him and, especially, I told them not to beat him ever again! In these situations, it is very important to remember that horses are prey animals and, when they are afraid and cannot escape, they get paralysed and cannot learn. Therefore, a terrified horse needs to be left alone so that he can learn. This is the reason why they should be let loose. He is afraid because he cannot run away. If, however, when he is taken to the coach he can actually run, as time goes by he will realise he does not need to run. But first, he needs to know he can leave, that is how his mind works. Horses are claustrophobic by nature, some of them more than others. There is no use in beating them because, in that way, fear is reinforced, it is like telling them: "You are right in being afraid, because you can die here."

During a course, a rider who was training with coaches said that, at a certain moment, the horse, which he himself said was wonderful, began galloping. He thought the horse did it to him on purpose and beat him. Until he realised that one of the wheels had got stuck and the horse solved the situation by galloping. Fortunately, during the course, this man recognised that horses do not do things in order to bother others, they do them for a reason. He became aware of this and shared the experience, and said, surprised: "I never thought horses did not do things on purpose, to bother us." We know how difficult it is to rule out this prejudice.

Horses are a perfect mirror of the riders

Horses are a perfect mirror of the riders

A functional concept is that of *working with the horse*, since the way in which we express our ideas conveys an intention and a more human type of relationship. Many people think they know how to ride a horse because they get onto the horse and make him gallop. Even though they may not be ill-intentioned, they have a mechanical and traditional idea of "mounting a horse", as if horses were cars or machines, in which you press the accelerator and make them run. Those who ride in this way, build a frustrating relationship, both for themselves and for the horse. I have seen so many jumping riders so tense, that they make their horses tense, and then say: "This horse is useless." They are very different from those relaxed riders, who create with their horses an artistic binomial, a unity.

An Eastern tale accurately describes this relationship of *unity*:

> *In order to smoothly ride a steed, it is essential to know*
> *how to direct the reins perfectly:*
> *When you should hold them back, do so.*
> *When you should slacken them, do so.*
> *When it is necessary to hold them back and slacken them, do so as well.*
> *The appropriate control of the reins is paramount for the steed and the rider to give their best, without any risks for any of them.*

Some time ago, I saw a beautiful jumping Anglo-Arabian mare. She was pure tension, excitement and anxiety. Such was her condition that she had trouble connecting with me when I started massaging her. Little by little, she started understanding and relaxed a little. The place where she had most tension was the lumbosacral area. Her horsewoman was not present; her mother came to see me instead. I told her: "Probably, the person who rides her is tense; her body language clearly indicates so." The lady answered: "That's right, my daughter gets very tense in her waist when she mounts her." The difficulty in these cases is to make the riders understand this and do something about it, because otherwise they end up thinking it is the horse's fault, when the horse is only responding to what the rider *teaches* him.

This beautiful mare felt pain also in her hocks, which was completely logical from a physical point of view, given the body posture of her horsewoman.

Horses perceive the different moods from people surrounding them; therefore, if they do not trust someone, they cannot respond appropriately. If there is negativity, they will be negative. They will do exactly as they are taught, either good or bad. If they get bored due to lack of motivation or leadership, they will try to save energy that will be useful in the future. Many people who rent horses say they are stupid because they do not want to move, but this is a sign of intelligence: they save energy, if they do not move, it is because they have no reason to do so.

Negative habits

Punishment, except in a few situations, reinforces negative habits instead of transforming them into positive ones. A very useful strategy is to avoid the situation in which the bad habit appears, or work in that situation until the horse learns a correct behaviour. For example, avoid giving him food when he bites the box's door, so that he goes through a period in which the habit does not appear, until it weakens. Working on the same situation until the negative habit is replaced by a positive one should be done in the case of an animal who shows his croup when we come near him; in such cases we need to insist several times, scaring him when he shows his croup so that he feels something unpleasant, and rewarding him when he shows his face, making him feel something pleasant.

One of the goals of training is to reduce the horses' instinctive responses: escape, distance, fight and fear; another goal is to stimulate natural positive responses: coming together, voluntary submission, collaboration, devotion and trust, thus creating useful habits, combining the different types of learning, together with what each horse adds himself, according to his personality and intelligence. Teaching has different levels, depending on where it is carried out. A primary level is where the horse lives, and a more complicated level is the real world, where he has to compete.

Working with horses' minds entails the possibility of anticipating their positive or negative reactions. In order to avoid negative behaviour, we must correct them at the slightest hint and teach them a positive habit. An example of this is the story of a very temperamental mare who, being sometimes the leader of her group, was used to showing her croup when other horses surrounded her. An assistant who was interested in this type of handling was working with her. When he started working, the mare tried to show him her croup, but when she was about to do it, he pushed her out, his entire body tense, like a feline, touching and frightening her, something unpleasant for the horse. She did it twice or three times, until she understood that that attitude was not necessary. Now she works in a positive way by playing and taking advantage of her vivacious and determined temperament. So, if she feels like expressing her inner self, she starts running, bucking a little to release tension, and then she keeps working, attentive and funny.

Obedience

Horses do as they are taught, be this correct or incorrect. An example of this is the case of an inattentive trainer who does not see when the horse makes a mistake during an exercise, and due to his lack of attention, does not correct him at that moment and the horse cannot know if he is doing the exercise rightly or wrongly. Finally, the inattentive trainer scolds and gets angry at the horse because he does not do the exercise right, when the problem is that he did not see the moment in which the horse made a mistake. A good trainer, besides being sensitive and attentive, should be humble enough to accept that he can make a mistake.

Chapter V

Another case is that of the mounted horse who is encouraged to move forward but, at the same time, he is not allowed to do so.

The best reward

The best reward for a horse is the *release of pressure*. Horses respond to pressure; therefore, when they are released simultaneously or immediately after doing the exercise, they understand and learn. When they are not released from pressure, they have no way of knowing they did the exercise right and, therefore, communication is interrupted. They keep trying to respond correctly but do not get the reward, the rider asks them for more and finally, the horse, who has responded correctly, ends up being punished (sometimes in a very cruel way).

Some trainers, who call this way of working *"Natural Horsemanship"*, suggest a series of useful and efficient concepts for working with horses, a sort of practical and functional philosophy.

Monty Roberts says:

- Ask yourself questions and avoid thinking that the horse wants to do the things wrong.

- Work with an open and flexible mind, without prejudices, in order to understand what is going on and how we can work it out.

- Consider all the options for every situation and choose the best one. Patience is a strategy when the aim is not achieved: let us try different options and avoid frustration. How can I improve myself so that my horse understands?

- Give the horse the benefit of the doubt. Think about the problem with the horse instead of reacting against him. Many times, they have things to say.

- Be consistent, that is, give them confidence and calm instead of scaring them.

- Create a pleasant environment to work in. The most important thing is that the place be calm and agreeable.

- People who work with horses should stand upright, have soft hands and good heart, always with the intention of doing what is best for the horse.

- Horses, by nature, will try to avoid conflicts but if there is a fight, they will fight more, since that is part of their survival instinct.

- Humans do not know everything, we make mistakes and we need to learn to learn and to improve. Sometimes, we are also negatively conditioned. We have the right to make mistakes and so does the horse.

- Every horse has different needs.
- A good trainer can hear what his horse tells him. A great trainer can hear a horse's whisper. Some horses are shouting and no one listens to them.
- A lot of people see, but cannot look.
- A great trainer is the one who makes the horse *want* to give a good performance.
- Horses should not be obliged to do anything.
- We need to pay a lot of attention to details.

Some old teachers say that the battle is won in the first step. Bear in mind that, when you start educating a horse, the most important thing is the first step.

Animal's condition

When training begins, it is necessary to know the horse's physical and mental state. If he comes from a stud farm where he was bred in fields, he will probably be well socialised with other horses and humans, will surely have received useful stimuli of life in nature and in the herd, will probably have had the chance of playing and making decisions; therefore, he will be a bright animal. On the other hand if he was bred locked in or alone, without having socialised, with few stimuli, he will probably be more easily frightened and hesitant and will have difficulties in learning, at least at the beginning. It is advisable to avoid working with a very stressed, anxious or excited animal, since he cannot pay attention. In this case, it is convenient to "decompress" him until he relaxes and can trust his trainer and pay him attention. This is very difficult to do with inhibited or frustrated horses; therefore, in such cases, it is useful to try to change their surrounding conditions, put them in a box with bars through which they can communicate with a neighbour, give them toys, or give them food more times a day, in order to recreate, as far as it is possible, their natural feeding behaviour. But the most important thing for a very frustrated or excited horse are activity and contact with others, even with a sheep or a cat, as is done in some places.

Attention factor

In order to learn, horses need to have reasons to pay attention. He will be motivated if his trainer is attentive and *present*, with all his senses focused on the situation with his horse. Since the horse grasps the different moods of his teacher, you can positively

Chapter V

Mutual attention is essential for training

influence him if you work with a positive attitude. At the beginning, it is difficult to work with a new horse in crowded places; therefore, we need to be patient until he "becomes accustomed" and is able to pay attention.

The same can happen if he feels attracted to something he likes. Young horses are curious by nature. Some good trainers allow them to pry into what they like, so that afterwards they can pay attention. Many times, this strategy is useful, since the horse gets what he wanted and then forgets about the object, animals or persons he felt attracted to. It is similar to what happens with children; *sometimes* you have to give them a candy. This will depend on the teacher's sensitivity, common sense and confidence, because if he is honest and efficient, he will be able to analyse how the horse works and how he teaches, without blaming the animal. This is called *anthropomorphic conditioning* (M. Worthington) and it implies that the trainer thinks about the horse's situation, and how he is teaching the horse instead of putting all the blame on the animal as if he were stupid. When a child does not understand a basic mathematics exercise, we do not hit him on the head and call him a fool. A good teacher thinks about how he can explain the exercise better so that he can understand it.

How do we avoid tension?

If a horse has difficulties understanding something, it is the teacher's responsibility to understand the situation and change what is necessary until the horse understands what he is asked to do. For example, if he is very tired or has made a great effort, once he has achieved something it is positive to finish the job cheerfully. If teaching is pleasant, then work and its results will also be pleasant. But, if the trainer gets bored, it will not work. Joy is contagious and, if the trainer is happy or in a good mood, the horse will feel it and will try to please more and more every time. We get optimal results when we learn with joy. It is beneficial to learn while we enjoy, so it is useful to take the time to watch and get to know the horse. Indians, who lived with their horses, spent a lot of time watching them; this is a useful time that helps us learn to think, elaborate strategies, ask ourselves questions and understand their world.

Responsible trainers

We know we have to be responsible for our actions and their consequences. Unfortunately, those who do not accept that they make mistakes can be very tough or strict with their horses, losing the chance of establishing a good relationship. It is unintelligent and very negligent to blame the horse or say that he is a fool or that he is not intelligent. There is a lot of information about learning processes, and about the different ways of solving difficulties. Therefore, if a trainer is incapable of examining himself in order to solve a difficulty and blames the horse as if he did it on purpose, he is avoiding his responsibility (M.Worthington).

Spontaneous answers

We can use spontaneous answers, such as when they voluntarily approach us, to show them how much we appreciate this kind of gesture. Gnomo learned by playing, because I used every little correct gesture to reward him. Every time he voluntarily came closer when he was loose, I congratulated him. Thus, he learned to come running when I got to the club, even if he was more than 200 meters away. And he always did it as if he were playing.

At the beginning of a training, a horse needs to receive continuous reinforcements every time he does something right, in order to make learning easier. But as training progresses, he must learn to work better every day, not always getting a reward. So you can work with the surprise factor, in order to eventually congratulate him, when he is not expecting it. In this way, you raise the positive reinforcement waiting threshold, because if it is too low, he will always be waiting for a reward but if it is high, he will do it voluntarily, because he trusts himself.

Many horses feel good when you congratulate them with your voice, with strokes or with a smile, at the same time as they are released from pressure. Releasing them from pressure is a primary reinforcement, whereas the sound, the strokes and the smile are secondary reinforcements. Some people say that the voice gives horses more confidence, especially if they are new. This secondary reinforcement facilitates

Chapter V

associations. Many riders "talk to" their horses or "whisper" to their horses during competitions.

What does observing the steps mean?

Breathing consists of different stages: inhalation–fullness–exhalation–emptiness. We cannot inhale again if we do not let the inspired air out. This process may be observed in ourselves. And it is a simple way of illustrating what observing the steps means. It is like walking, it is not possible to take a step without having finished taking the previous one; therefore, it is functional to work with small goals. When the first one is achieved, the animal is rewarded and moves on to the next goal. Only when he achieves it is he rewarded, and so on. According to some researchers, every new knowledge is stored at a neuronal union so, in a way, the horse becomes more intelligent.

When you work with patience, observing the steps, with small goals and for short periods, horses will learn different exercises in a short period of time.

Sevillana, the mare who plays. Her sister Jazmín sniffs at her, as if she was asking: "what are you doing? Where were you?"

The mare who was working with my assistant lived in freedom, was determined and "liked to argue a little." She needed to be well treated, consistently and firmly, but "with some games involved". If the assistant worked with tension, she responded with tension and anger. But, if he was very relaxed, she would try to dominate the situation. On the contrary, when he worked as if they were "playing", the result was excellent. He used his body language to play with her, so that she paid attention and stayed focused.

The game distracted her and she forgot to organise her group. It was interesting because she would sometimes bend the neck and get bigger, so he acted as a mirror and got bigger, then she calmed down and they continued working. It was as if he were telling her: "if you get bigger, I get even bigger." It seems that she felt supported when he responded in that way. When he mounted her, she responded perfectly to his voice and was very obedient. Many times, when he finished his job he would let her loose in the paddock with other mares of her group, and take another horse to work with him. After a round, she went to the pen's door and stared at him while he was working with the other horse. It was interesting that she did not leave and stayed there, observing.

The useful effort

Resting, entertainment and going for a walk are useful activities that help decompress the mind. It is good for the horse to enjoy and forget about work until he is ready to go back to the training. As we previously saw, there is a latent learning that takes place when necessity appears or in certain circumstances. An exercise might not work one day, but it might on another. When we practice again, we first remind the horse of what he does correctly and then move on to the next objective. It is a tactic related with patience and the result is that, in general, when he exercises again he does it better than last time. It is essential to recognise the moment in which the effort is useful: when you can demand something from the horse and when you have to stop. Why would you demand a new and perfect exercise when he had not yet incorporated it in his mind? If one demands too much, we run the risk of boring him.

Gnomo put his entire soul to understand and asked more and more every time. I used to let him play a lot and I think he loved it; he could practice his abilities, coordinate himself and had a great connection with his own body. He was strong and determined. If I had repressed him or demanded too much of him, he would not have shown his potential.

Chapter V

Intuition

Intuition is the voice of the heart, the inner self or the essential being. We want the horse to be willing to work for us because he likes to. There is mutual respect because there is real friendship, where everyone has his own place and his function is well defined.

Intuitive communication produces a subtle, functional and honest exchange. They can help us find that quality in ourselves.

When is punishment effective?

There are moments in which a punishment simultaneous with the action might be effective for teaching purposes, like when a colt or an adult horse bites. In that case, it is necessary to slap them or put a hand above their eyes, being careful not to hurt them. Why? Because this will produce an impact that will leave them thinking about the consequences of their actions before doing it again. In social life, limits are set and in this particular case, punishment would emulate that of a horse towards a young colt who would invade his personal sphere, and he will respond with a menace or biting him if the colt does not react to that threat.

Many times, horses are punished and do not understand the reason, such as when they refuse to jump. If the animal is punished after having refused to do it, he does not understand the reason and finally associates the whole situation with fear and punishment, but he does not learn. If he refuses to jump, it is necessary to know all the previous circumstances: Does he feel any pain? Is he afraid? Has he been hit in order to jump? Have nails been put in the hooves' bandages so he can raise them and avoid touching the fence? Does he like to jump? and if he does, is he afraid of certain obstacles? If he feels fear or insecurity, he might be stimulated with a firm voice or being gripped more strongly with the legs before jumping, to make him feel secure. You ask him a little more and you are confident he will respond; as soon as he does what you asked him to, it is very important to reward him. In this situation we also work with small goals, repeating the exercise so he can overcome fear, mental block or lack of enthusiasm. It is very important to be precise when the reinforcement is used, which means that it is necessary to anticipate the horse's reaction, a split second before or at the same moment, to prevent him from doing something undesired.

Gestalt thinking

The horse's mind perceives every situation in a complete way. This means that he might learn a lesson and then forget it in another context because the whole situation has changed.

Due to this natural ability of the horse, it is useful to introduce new stimuli in each situation to keep him alert and so he can provide new responses or modify negative habits. For example, it is correct to take a horse who is accustomed to jumping in his place, to another place; in this way, certain data to which he is accustomed are modified. When the situation changes, attention, self-confidence and coordination are stimulated. If we learn to observe the whole situation, the whole image, we will see which factor or factors can be modified in order to improve or enrich the situation.

It is not out of a whim that the horse stops doing something that he usually does correctly. What has changed in the situation? Is it possible that he is feeling pain or has been hurt? Or is there a negative memory or any change in the environment?

Why do many people get angry with their horses?

Some people who are "experts on horses" feel frustrated, angry or embarrassed when things go wrong. It is paradoxical because many of these people deny the fact that horses have emotions or are intelligent but, when they undergo these situations, they treat horses as if they were people who were trying to hurt them or project in the animals their own failures or difficulties. When they do this, the situation gets complicated even if they are not willing to accept it. Unfortunately, others take their frustration, fear or negativity out on their horses.

In relation to this "Neanderthal" functioning, there is a story written by Nasrudin, a writer who lived in the Middle East during the XIV century and taught lessons with humour, which illustrates this situation:

> *A philosopher had taken an appointment with Mulla Nasrudin.*
> *But when he came at the appointed time, Nasrudin was out.*
> *He became angry and wrote "Stupid" on Nasrudin's door and went back.*
> *When Nasrudin returned he saw this and went to the philosopher and told him "I feel very sorry, I forgot the appointment. But, I recalled it as soon as I saw your signature on my door. It was so thoughtful of you"*

Horses, noble and shy animals, help us know our inner selves and accept our own fears, deficiencies, or incorrect patterns, and also help us learn about unity, humbleness, humility, devotion, and to connect ourselves with our spirit. Efficient techniques of body work and meditation are fundamentally based on teaching the correct way of breathing that allows us to improve our functioning, thus avoiding the trap of compulsive and inefficient mechanisms. These are effective techniques to observe and think in a useful way about the situations in which we are involved. If a person knows he might become violent at work, it is possible to avoid this reaction by taking a deep breath so as to detach from the situation and visualise acting with dignity. It is a matter of *common sense and dignity*. If trainers are tense or in a bad mood, they might unfairly mistreat the horse. We are not that important, that is the reason why we should not take ourselves so seriously.

The excess of pressure and tension is harmful. I remember a racing mare who was terrified as soon as she got into the starting gate because she had had a terrible accident where she almost lost her life. We worked with her together with a person who rehabilitated abused horses. At first, the mare felt too much pressure, so it was difficult to get into her world. So we decided to change the method and give her massages. When she got the massages, she relaxed and began to trust; therefore, it was possible to start "communicating with her." We took her to a round pen where she could run and relieve body tension. We finally made her eat near the starting gate. That was a huge step for her because she ended up eating at only a meter from the starting gate, something unthinkable for the people who worked with her. They said that until that day, they could not get her closer than 10 meters because she was terrified.

We worked this way with the mare without knowing that somebody has called this method *passive leadership*.

A frightened, tense, nervous horse cannot "think", he is not capable of learning and the last thing he needs is to be pressured. These horses need time to be able to trust. They need to relieve body and mental tension, to gain confidence, feel their own body. Passive leadership has very good results because horses end up trusting the "passiveness" of the person they are working with.

What is passive leadership?

During the first encounter between a horse and a human being, the horse will try to understand who this stranger is by means of his own reference of social life. He has to learn to live in this new "herd" led by man. The herd consists of all members: mares of different ages, the stallion, the foals, the fillies, and the youngest ones. There is an alpha leader and, between this leader and the periphery, there are progressive levels of hierarchy. This means that in the middle, we can find the passive leaders, those animals who are simply trying to be in harmony with the rest, who have no interest in competing for leadership because they are fine with their position and function. The other horses feel at ease with them because they are calm in their daily activities. Most horses need calm; so they can save energy, avoid conflict and, naturally, want to spend more time with those who make less trouble; therefore, they avoid contact with very aggressive people or horses. Passive leaders cause minimum stress because they are peaceful in their actions: they hardly use force and apparently lead by example: wherever they go, the others want to go.

Mark Rashid, an American trainer, who proposed the concept of *passive leadership*, related an experience with mustang horses who had to be captured to be given to someone else. At that moment, they did not take into account certain factors. They had to work fast in order to be able to deliver them. As a result, horses had

An example of passive leadership with Belsebú in El Solitario, province of Bueonos Aires.

difficulties in understanding what they were being asked to do, and they could not retain something simple. Trainers redefined the task and arrived at the conclusion that the reason why the horses had so many difficulties in learning was that they were overloaded with information, they were anxious, tense and mainly terrified.

They were *disoriented* because they went through a lot in such a short time: their lives had completely changed, they lost their usual way of living. The structure they kept in their herd no longer existed and, in its place, there was a group of people trying to tell them which type of horses they should become. These thoughts enabled them to change the working methods during the second year, when they tried something completely different. When they arrived, instead of launching a training plan, they first *"decompressed"* them. *They were given time* to get accustomed to the environment without putting the halters on, while they tried to imitate a structure similar to that of their herd in daily activity. They put the mustangs in separate paddocks but allowed them to see each other so they did not feel lonely. They implemented a strict nutrition programme, which consisted of giving them food at the same time. They also cleaned the paddocks at the same time every day. The plan was to give the horses something to create a daily relation with food or cleaning, a routine. Once they arrived, when the sun came out, somebody brought them food. When the sun was high, somebody went to clean. When the sun began to go down, somebody brought them more food. So they created habits.

During the first 10 days, the mustangs moved away, ran to the other side of the paddock when someone tried to approach them. The following week, they looked nervously and inquisitively but were less scared of people who visited them. Around the third week, they began to accept them and, at times, they were so calm that one managed to start working with them. Not all the horses were ready to work. It took longer with some. But when training began, their mental state was better than that of the first group and they could understand what they were being taught.

The *essential thing* was that during the first three weeks they worked in a way that is not considered training. But that "non-training" marked the difference in preparing them for the future. Because in that way, they could learn to trust, they relaxed and began to regard people as reliable beings. Trainers centred the focus of attention in keeping that confidence once it was established. Three things that helped most to keep confidence were: being quiet, consistent and available the whole time, a similar attitude to that of the passive leaders that the horses chose.

This kind of work with horses is similar to what country people do: for many days, they familiarise themselves with horses loose in fields until they begin to trust those who feed them and give them water. People become part of the group. Horses incorporate their smell, postures, and way of acting; they store that information in their long-term memory and therefore, people become part of their lives, routines and group; in other words, *they get accustomed*. In a way, it is a working philosophy that takes into account the horses' needs and lifestyle.

Those who have rigid ideas or great expectations about what a horse is supposed to do, run the risk of using force to obtain results. And strength is brutality, it has nothing to do with dignity. When the horse loses confidence in you, he is lost forever. The horse who is confident, respects us the way he naturally does with his peers. When a horse's body language is misunderstood, certain actions might be interpreted as lack of respect, for example: when he is running in a round pen and kicks at a person, a conduct that might be defensive or might arise due to confusion. He might react that way out of fear, because he wants to play or because he does not understand what he is being asked to do. Or it may be in self defense, to release an excess of energy, a reaction to something we have done or due to the memory of a stressful incident. Therefore, it is a sign of intelligence to "see" the reason that he is doing it.

Dr. M. Kiley-Worthington is doing research with the ability of horses and other species' to understand certain words. The following are part of her conclusions:

"It is possible to challenge the preconceived notions about teaching and learning in horses. If we think about it this way, it is possible to change and improve considerably the speed of learning and what they learn. Horses will learn to respond to verbal orders and will also learn the meaning of at least some words, not only orders. Like 'up' and 'down', 'inside' and 'outside', some adjectives, verbs and nouns. Fear and dominance are not necessary if we want to teach them some tasks quickly. Objectively speaking, emotional ties and 'liking' each other accelerate the learning process. Verbal and visual praise signals can be important reinforcements so they should be used in the adequate context – not at random – so that they obtain meaningful results. Equines and other species learn to imitate their human teachers' behaviour and this might be used as an important aid when teaching. Horses, just like us, like to feel they are liked."

The real artist keeps the animal's beauty and spirit alive and leads those qualities to its full potential. Many years ago, a veterinarian treated a small racing mare, who was not beautiful and did not have a good conformation, but was excellent running the 1,600 meters. She was unbeatable! Why? Because her trainer saw her capacity and did not reject her for being imperfect and this combination helped the little mare win international classics. Another art story with the horse was published in a specialised equine magazine: a rider was attracted to a neighbour's horse. One day he saw they were putting him on a truck and he asked what they were going to do with him, and they answered that they were taking him to the slaughterhouse! The rider bought the horse and the animal ended up being a great horse at international jumping competitions! Another story, which happened in Buenos Aires, was that of a man who bought a carthorse with which he competed in jumping up to 1.10 meters high, with very good results.

SOME ASPECTS OF THE WORK WITH FOALS

What is early stimulation?

The idea is to make foals experience all the possible situations that they will encounter in their adult life. The muzzle, the halter, walking over surfaces that make them feel unsteady, like the ones they will use when getting into a vehicle. To get them accustomed to different noises: cars, trucks, plastic bags, applause; certain manoeuvers like being injected, bathed, examined by the veterinarian; seeing shiny objects like a plastic bag or even to have something over the back, like a small blanket that imitates what will be a saddle in the future. It is best to stimulate them with the greatest amount of possible situations because, the more varied the situations, the more abilities they will develop.

Chapter V

"Me? Curious?"

As we previously saw, the first months of life are an excellent time to transmit to horses the necessary information for the future. The experiences they undergo during those months will affect them for the rest of their lives, for better or worse. It is best for them to learn, as soon as possible, man's laws, since they will have to live with them. Foals who are early stimulated behave really well during their adult life.

They easily adapt to different situations and are easy to handle, because they trust man, especially when he is good to them. The type of work done with each foal depends on whether he is naturally a follower who needs more confidence, or a leader who needs firmness.

At the moment, some foals raised by a group of students from the Faculty of Veterinary at Casilda, Santa Fe province, are running races. These foals were trained by them since the day they were born

The first months of life they were in close contact. They worked following certain norms of behaviour with the idea of getting easy-to-handle horses. When they got to the stud where they began the training, they quickly adapted to their new lives and people responsible for this new phase were happy to have well educated foals. One of them is running with very good results, he has already won some competitions, and jockeys' comments are related to his tameness and easiness to handle.

Familiarisation

Familiarisation is related to habituation. The young people who raised the foals used to walk inside the corral, talking to them without upsetting them, carefully, so that the foals got familiarised with them, got accustomed to their presence, incorporated them as part of their social group.

Foals are naturally curious and want to know new and strange things. Some are more reckless than others, depending on their personality, and are more likely to get

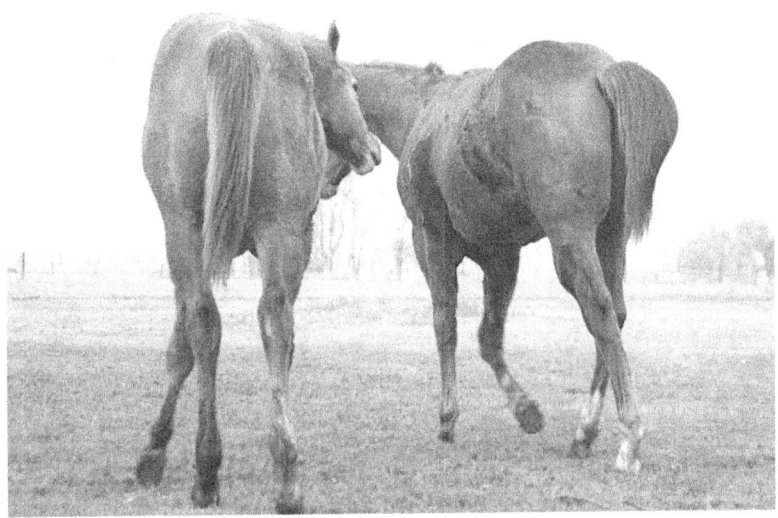

Pictures 32, 33 and 34: Quarter mile foals from *Quebracho Herrado* stud farm practicing their rituals.

Pictures 35, 36, 37 and 38: Games are necessary. They compensate for aggression and fear instincts.

closer to certain people. When they get closer, it is useful to let them sniff you, you reach out your hand as far as they let you, that is to say, being available, as when a human baby wants to investigate a person. But it is best to prevent them from licking the hands to excess so they do not get accustomed to invading your personal sphere or bite you when playing. Foals, like adult horses, feel at ease when the environment is calm and quiet, so it is good to avoid shouting or frightening them because then, it will be necessary to work with them to overcome fear and make them trust you again.

At that age, bones are very delicate; therefore it is necessary to protect them, especially the nape of the neck articulation because any effort in this articulation might cause lifelong damage. Sensitive and nervous-motor information, which intervenes in the balance, coordination and equilibrium of the horse, passes through this articulation. That is the reason why, when you teach the foal to be haltered and led, you should do it tenderly so as to avoid hurting his neck and the nape of the neck articulation. During the first days of life, it is very easy to teach him to follow you, give you their hooves and be cleaned.

If it is not possible to work with the foal during the first months, you can put on a little muzzle and a soft halter later on, and let him use them for short periods of time so he can get used to them. In this way, when he steps on the halter he learns that if he removes the leg, it loosens, so he learns to give in. Every manoeuver is performed calmly, softly and patiently, to avoid scaring him and so the handling becomes another part of his daily life. Some people teach them to be haltered during weaning because, as he feels lonely and insecure, he needs to follow somebody who protects him. The difference between foals who have been stimulated at an early age and those who have not, is striking; the latter are terrified when they undergo these situations for the first time.

You can brush their mane, first as a game, near their mother, until they get accustomed to be completely cleaned. In order to give them a bath, it is best to start with water softly running over their hooves, not with a strong stream, with circular movements like massages, and then later wash the whole body slowly. The idea is to make all those manoeuvers agreeable. It is useful to accustom them by putting a wet hand over their head and then, little by little, moving on gently to a hose without scaring them, without pressing them too much, until they get accustomed and allow us to advance a little more.

In order to mount a horse, it is advisable to let him loose by his mother's side. If you put on a muzzle and a halter, you have to work by their side and if he gets scared, you immediately let him loose. Although at the beginning he might be daunted by the contact with the halter, once he gets accustomed to feel it between his legs, he will soon stand still and wait.

Chapter V

Due to the fact that young animals can only pay attention for a while, it is best to work for short periods, from 10 to 15 minutes. When he does something correctly, he is rewarded and allowed to rest. Being freed from exercise is a reward. This kind of exercise can be done with foals of 5 or 6 months old. When previous and subsequent experiences to weaning are positive, training will be much easier.

It is not practical to tie them to the tethering post because during the first years of life their bones are not ossified, so they run the risk of hurting themselves. They may even kill themselves, because those foals that are easily scared begin to pull until they finally break their necks.

Games stimulate intelligence

The impulse of the game responds to the play instinct that mammals and birds have. The game is a necessity and also a way of compensating the fear and aggression instincts. Every foal that has his basic needs guaranteed – nutrition and security – "will learn to play." The ritual game stimulates him to develop prey and socialisation instincts and also to be part of the herd. The foal who plays, is training for the different contingencies of life, he stays alert, learns to learn, develop his potential and it is also possible that he develops "creative" abilities, because he might create an unusual habit for his species. In every species there is an animal who has an intelligence above average; those are the ones about whom people have stories. Once they are domesticated and have the chance of expressing their play instinct and communication with man, they experience unusual situations for their species, which causes them to try to solve different situations from the ordinary ones. The game is a manifestation of freedom, joy and wellbeing; therefore, it is essential for the existence of animals.

Game functions

- Development of coordination.
- Development of the sensory perception system.
- Learning of adequate reactions.
- Development of self-confidence.
- Socialisation.

When a foal meets another foal or an adult horse, he puts into practice his way of expression and learns to interpret the other. During the first months, the foal is too attached to his mother, but as he grows, especially the male horse, he is more reckless and curious. When he gets closer to adults, they put him in his place and teach him to respect the body space. If he grows up in a group where there are other foals, dynamic relations develop, in which the bravest dominates the most submissive. Those who are raised in herds with animals of different ages are more relaxed when they start training than those who are raised in groups separated by age, because they have more and different opportunities to practice. In wild life, weaning takes place at the age of 9 months, the moment at which the animal starts to get on with his own life; this is a natural weaning which does not produce stress and, if it does, is less than an artificially caused stress.

The case of a filly who did not socialise

During a course, a student brought his mare with her filly. The filly, who was quite lively, had only had contact with his mother and owners. As these people were learning to treat horses, they were not clear about the way they should educate her. The filly was intrusive because she did not know the rules of equine behaviour. One day there were a few loose mares and the filly got too close to them, without knowing she could be rejected, and that is exactly what happened: one of the mares kicked her badly. The owner and the filly got really scared. But an hour later, many horses got closer and she had a more careful attitude and only approached to a distance from which she could not be kicked. Although the experience was hard, she learned something. It is worth mentioning Xenophon's words:

> *You should never shout at a horse with anger or a feeling of burden.*
> *If he does something wrong, it is because he does not understand.*

CHAPTER VI

INTELLIGENCE AND LEADERSHIP

Mares and Foals with a Sheepdog (John Emms, 18th -19th C)

My kingdom for a horse.
W. SHAKESPEARE

What an expression of intelligence this mare shows having just finished playing polo!

WHAT IS INTELLIGENCE?

It is the ability to solve different situations using the tools we have in the best possible way. Intelligence – or lack of it – is observed in the actions of an individual. It is not a physical thing but several powers that complement each other. Usually, intelligence is wrongly interpreted as the knowledge or the amount of information that a person has, when these are actually socially constructed activities.

There is another Nasrudin tale, when he was ferrying some travellers, which illustrates this point:

> *Nasrudin was ferrying a very demanding traveller across a broad river. As they began crossing, the scholarly traveller asked if the voyage would be very rough, Nasrudin made a minor grammatical error in his answer.*
>
> *The traveller remarked, "You, who wears a turban and calls himself a Mulla, have you ever studied grammar?"*
>
> *"No," Nasrudin admitted.*
>
> *"Well then," the traveller replied, "you have wasted half of your life!"*

Chapter VI

Jasmín, from La Purísima.

Several minutes later a terrible storm started and the small boat began to fill with water, Nasrudin turned to the traveller and asked, "Have you ever learned how to swim?"

"No," the traveller responded.

"Well then," Nasrudin replied, "you have wasted all your life... we are sinking!"

Those who ignore individual intelligence and teach in a uniform and mechanical way, without evaluating the individual capacity of each animal and the *circumstances*, do not see the potential of many animals.

Why do we talk about the intelligence of horses?

We do this is in order to understand how it works and establish efficient communication. There is a word that defines this type of relationship: empathy. Empathy is a person's feeling of emotional involvement in another person's reality, that is, the capacity to share the other person's situation, or to feel what the other person feels; therefore, empathy enables us to understand horses and foresee their actions. *Thus, it is useful to look and see their world from their own perspective.* Those people who have the ability to learn to think "with their horses", not only foresee their reactions but also take advantage of the best of them.

Their nature

As we have already mentioned, horses are mammals who live in a group –the herd– and who have a communication system based on corporal, chemical and vocal signals, with very clear and precise coexistence rules they naturally abide by. Therefore, their way of relating to man is natural and logical from their perspective, since man becomes part of the herd, with the hierarchy of leader if the relationship between them is correctly established.

Their characteristics and abilities - According to Robert Miller DVM

- Their fast, high-speed flight is their primary survival behaviour.
- Their perception is extremely acute.
- They have a desensitisation capacity due to habit-forming (habituation).
- Their memory is infallible, for positive as well as for negative things.
- Horses' intelligence and leadership
- They have a great ability to differentiate what is dangerous from what is not.
- They live in a hierarchical system with a clear and consistent leadership; therefore, they are easily trainable, if you know how to do it.
- They exercise dominance and establish hierarchies controlling their own movement and direction over their mates.
- Their body language is clear for the species.
- They are a precocious species. Their foals are born completely fit and able to run only a few hours after their birth.
- They need stability: clear habits and unchanging rules.
- They have a great capacity of adaptation.
- They learn very quickly in their natural life.
- They avoid conflicts in order to save energy that might be useful in the future.
- They are noble and loyal.

Horses are shy and cautious creatures, two characteristics which allow them to survive in different places, environments and climates, and their reactions are in tune with their reality because, otherwise, they would make mistakes that could cost them their lives. It is due to this survival need that their mind functions as a *gestalt* – configuration, form, essence - as we saw in previous chapters. This term refers to horses' natural ability to take *all the information from the situation in which they are.*

They need to *differentiate* the subtle stimuli and the details of the environment through their sharp sense of observation, in order to evaluate whether there is danger or not; this ability allows them to live in peace, because if they were not able to differentiate, they would live permanently tense or running away. They are very good at knowing their territory and always remember the necessary details for their life. If we measure intelligence by the speed of learning, then horses are brilliant, because they can remember situations they have only lived once, especially if there is an emotional component in them.

Regarding their sense of observation and their ability to read the environment and solve a situation, we have the case of the mare who prepared her mud bath, shown in Chapter IV - Learning, who is a good example of this.

Another example is that of a farm labourer's grandfather who worked in Cordoba, and had his workhorse. We know how important horses are for country people - we have heard many stories about horses taking their sleeping riders back home at night. But the peculiarity of the story is that this horse, as well as taking the sleeping rider back home, opened every gate he had to go through.

David Broome, worldwide jumping champion, says: "My Welsh Mountain pony is like a wizard: he knows exactly where to stand in order to walk out of the door when some horse is taken out, leaving us no chance of stopping him; in other words, he tries to use one of his tools, moving fast, to solve the problem of moving to the other side. He also jumps out of the stable if it is physically possible. But if he cannot use his hooves he improvises and tries to untie himself grabbing, the halter with his mouth. Who can deny that if he had hands, he would instantly open the door? He sees the problem: 'I want to be in another place', and knows the solution: 'I have to go through the door or untie the knot', but he lacks the appropriate physical means to put the solution into practice. He does the best he can and many times he succeeds."

These are real examples, not artificial ones, that clearly show how horses "manage themselves" when they want to get something they need.

Hierarchy and submission – biological function

In order to satisfy their needs, horses developed a group hierarchy system, which entails the existence of dominance and submission, with the variations in between. In everyday life, every structure and behaviour has a purpose and a function. Life in a group has benefits when compared to life in isolation. Groups offer safety and protection, and enable more animals to eat more food, in an efficient way. But in order to live in a group, there are some rules that need to be observed and sometimes there are rival situations when there is shortage of food and water, or when there are not enough mates to procreate.

In this system, every animal naturally takes its place within the group, because they instinctively know that everyone has a function, and this poses no psychological contradictions for them.

When the leader is strong and consistent, the group usually lives in equilibrium, since the other members are calm as they accept the permanent features of the environments. This system is so precise and respected by all members of the group that even submissive and threatening attitudes have their own signals. What are they?

When an animal is submissive, he avoids visual contact, walks backwards, puts his head downwards and tries to look "innocent." When an animal looks threatening, he puts his ears flat against the back of his neck, stretches his facial muscles, enlarges his body and shows his teeth. Between these two attitudes, there is a wide range of intermediate expressions.

LEADERSHIP

Leadership is shared. The stallion is in charge of serving the mares, being careful not to lose them, getting them organised, throwing out the foals who are ready to serve and the fillies with whom he does not want to leave descendants. The leading mare, or the oldest mare, on the other hand, is in charge of breeding and teaching, she is the one who leads the group to the places where they can find food and water, and the one who decides when to move. Mares learn to live together in harmony. Stallions are highly communicative and active; they are "workers." Their entire physiology is suited for communication and contact.

When the leader grows older, gets weak or sick, the herd loses the stability it needs and the animals who are close to the hierarchical scale grow anxious; conflicts appear, until a new leader is found. The herd suffers when there is instability. Since hierarchy is a dynamic fact, a strong horse might try to become the leader, in terms of the group's need of stability. But if the leader can still act as such, the defiant horse accepts it and retires.

It is possible to recreate a positive environment for them, imitating the features of their wild life. Since their hierarchy and submission system is biological if, in the relationship with men, the hierarchy is not clear and they feel they are on the same scale, they get unsettled and feel insecure. How do they express this? Through anxiety, excitement, minor threats, invasion of personal spaces, rush; all of these reactions appear out of frustration and insecurity.

Unfortunately, sometimes these reactions are not correctly understood, causing many horses to develop behavioural disorders and in turn, to be ill-treated.

Horses who live in pastures or fields and grow up together, or in herds put together by man, in which sometimes there is a lot of mobility, create subtle and sometimes changing hierarchies. I am working with a group of Anglo-Hispanic mares who have lived together ever since they were born. The group is made up of: Incamar, a racing thoroughbred, the eldest and the mother of all of them. Then we have, in this order: Jazmín, 7 years old; Purita, 6 years old; Sevillana, 5 years old; who are all daughters of the same Andalusian stallion. Then we have Alicia and Malvina, daughters of Incamar

Chapter VI

and another Andalusian stallion. The last one to form the group is Clavelito, a gelding who takes care of the mares and is a close friend of theirs. They are very supportive of each other; *e. g.*, when dogs get into their corral, they get together and run after them. Even though Incamar is the eldest one and the first one to eat and drink, leadership is variable, depending on the circumstances. On the same field there is another stallion who lives in a different pasture; when they are more or less close, if Jazmin sees him coming closer, she runs to the fence, approaches him and squeals. So, Jazmin is in charge of keeping the stallion away, or investigating where some noises come from. I realised that when I mounted her. If there are strange noises and I let her go wherever she wants, even though she gets scared, she walks where she can hear and see where the noise comes from. She is like a sentry-guard. For other decisions, there is Sevillana, the third one. She is the soul of the group; sometimes she leads the group or, when she sees people, she finds out what is going on. Now that my mare had a little foal, she takes care of him and stays near him. She also chases Purita and my filly – the ones in the periphery of the group – whom she moves away from when someone gets into the paddock or when the food arrives. Purita, the 6-year-old one, holds the position of less hierarchy together with my 2-year-old filly who joined the group a few months ago. Alicia and Malvina are very close friends and no wonder, since they are both daughters of the same stallion. But when it comes to food, Alicia, the largest one, dominates and handles her sisters. They only respect their mother.

In the following pictures, we can see some of the group dynamics.

The herd: at the back, Clavelito, the gelding, next to Incamar, his inseparable partner. Jazmín, the group's sentry, observes us.

The closest one is Sevillana; at the back is Purita and, behind her, Malvina.

Intelligence And Leadership

Sevilla throws Nasruddina out.

Sevillana comes to communicate with me. What is going on?

Purita and Nasruddina. Sevillana took them to this spot. They are the peripherals of the group.

According to some research, when there is instability, the functioning of the immune and gastrointestinal systems and fecundity are affected. Also horses get hurt, fight over food and water and are in permanent conflict, some have difficulty in gaining weight, even if they are well fed. When one of these horses is taken to a place with a more efficient handling, he quickly gains weight.

What are the advantages of the hierarchical system?

For the mares of highest hierarchy, there are better chances of choosing places with the best food and water, and better chances of being near the stallion, in order to procreate. Thus, their foals have better growth chances, since they are born in a period in which they can efficiently feed. This system is so well established that some mares pretend to be in heat during winter, in order to get the stallion to serve them and prevent him from going with some new mare. This is precisely what happened with Incamar, who made Haram serve her when a foaled and pregnant mare arrived at her place, in the middle of the winter.

What is the function of dominance?

Dominant mares tend to give birth to foals who imitate their behaviour. For example, if the mother is dominant towards the others, the foal learns to be dominant because he is protected by her, and learns to take his place on the hierarchical ladder. Some dominance features and the ability to run – flight response – are seen in modern racing horses again, since there might be a positive correlation, especially in mares, between the ability to run and dominance.

Small, artificial, stacked or unstable populations are prone to higher aggression levels during their activities such as eating, drinking or receiving someone. There is a descending drip-like effect, from the leader towards the periphery, in which the leader threatens the following one, who, in turn, does the same with the second one and so on. It is possible to observe this phenomenon in groups of loose horses in small paddocks, in which hierarchy is not clear, and in which there is a lot of mobility, since horses come in and out every week. But there are groups of passive, peripheral or submissive animals, who wait for their turn and go to eat and drink when the others have finished, without fighting.

This descendant effect of aggression is called "redirected aggression".

This type of behaviour is sometimes observed in pairs of animals, in which one of them is dominant and takes it out on the other one, be it a horse, a dog or a person; but this is not always the case, since there are pairs of horses who have peaceful relations, with a subtle, dynamic or not completely established dominance. Many of these pairs of horses develop a behavioural disorder called "separation anxiety", because they cannot tolerate being separated from their mates.

What is the function of submission?

The hierarchical system is related to order and obedience; therefore, submission is a biological feature that favours the group's survival. It is easy to realise when there is submission and when there is not.

Those who work with some corporal therapy technique know that horses calm down when you help them gradually to lower their head. This movement, which they learn at an early age, implies an association of low head with calm and raised head with alarm or excitement. As we saw in the chapter devoted to language, a raised head is related to alarm and a low head to relaxation.

Do horses make decisions?

In my country there is a well-known technique, developed over many years, for breeding the thoroughbred, a horse kept "in fields." These horses spend the first part of their lives "in the wild", getting used to inclement weather and to different grounds. Even very good breeders have their foals, who then become champions, in places where winter is very harsh. They get used to "looking out for themselves", that is, they learn to "make decisions" regarding their well-being. They are always stimulated.

In order to make decisions, there must be motivations: signals from mates, information about the territory, signals from other animals, and other sensory stimuli, such as hunger or thirst.

Therefore, when a horse is trained, he uses a motivation: "to please his trainer", because he imitates what he does inside his group when he tries to please others or when he tries to avoid a conflict with the leader.

Stimuli reach the brain, where they are quickly processed. Using his common sense, the horse analyses the data from previous experiences stored in his memory, and answers: with a movement, a body signal, or a feeling of approach, rejection or fear. In education, motivations and positive feelings are used, in order to transform them into the grounds for other motivations, aiming at making the animal want to voluntarily do what he is asked to. Pleasant things motivate learning; unpleasant things block and hinder learning, and the horse can suffer so much that he might develop behavioural disorders. He is not foolish; he is like us: the more pleasant the things we do, the more motivated we are and the better we will do our job.

How do they use stimuli?

The different types of stimulus are classified and differentiated by external and internal senses. The brain receives a message, in a specific area for each stimulus, and distinguishes whether it is useful or not; *e.g.* this allows the horse to differentiate noises: a mate calling him, food, and the alarm. He disregards the non-dangerous data, especially if he has another priority, like eating, but if the data indicates danger, he will flee even if he is hungry.

Do they feel frustration?

Yes - for example when they feel attraction and fear of something at the same time, which may happen with young and curious horses, or when they do not know the place. Gestures seem to indicate that: "I'd like to get closer to that object, but I'm afraid." Or when they are tied and cannot eat or free themselves, or come into contact with another horse, they express frustration through restlessness, anxiety and pawing in order to get what they want. Other times, they get anxious when they go for a ride and move apart from their friends. In this case, the rider should be able to motivate him so that the horse pays attention and work becomes his priority.

Horses with low frustration tolerance might develop displacement behaviours or stereotypes to ease conflict. Confinement does not offer options and they become disturbed. In many stud farms, they keep stallions locked up during hours without allowing physical or visual contact with other horses. The poor stallions, who smell receptive mares whom they cannot see, become literally "neurotic", they get sick. The least they can do is to get sick. The same happens to people confined who are not allowed to communicate with other people. As they cannot channel their natural and physiological energy, horses kick, walk restlessly, move to and fro, eat wood, swallow air or get colic, for example.

This kind of artificial handling can also stress horses, something that happens, for example, in clubs at feeding time. In a natural state, horses eat most of the day, around 16 hours in total. The usual alimentary routine in riding clubs consists of two meals a day, something completely different from their natural alimentary behaviour. Horses who, in free conditions, eat over such a long time, under these circumstances, get bored waiting for someone to let them out, clean them or just talk to them; so, eating time is a deeply-rooted habit for them and when this time arrives (remember they have an indicator in their stomach that sends a signal whenever they feel hungry), they are so anxious that they sweat or kick, and some get so excited that they move to and fro or neigh constantly.

Displacement behaviours follow normal conduct patterns at first, but then become exaggerated, as in the horse who walks in the box when he is about to be fed, a natural behaviour because they normally walk and stare at others when they eat, therefore, walking is part of the eating process. They only exaggerate in those cases. For this reason, horses who live in boxes eat facing outwards and, although they "waste" food, it is normal for them. At some studs at the racetracks, it is possible to see alfalfa hanging out of the box, beside the windows, so that horses can eat facing outwards. It is a clever solution.

Stimuli and responses

Every individual classifies stimuli and vital experiences in a "personal", unique way. Their responses will be a combination of an "instinctive" tendency and learning. Every animal has different tactics and ways of acting according to their personality, genes and the circumstances in which they were raised and educated. Some will be more skilful than others.

Intelligence And Leadership

We might define the preservation instinct as the combination of norms of behaviour that are genetically transmitted, whose function is the preservation of the individual and the life of the species: "There is a predator, we have to flee." The main characteristic of instinct is that horses' reactions are rigid, efficient, without liberty to chose or decide. *Flee first, then think.* Stabled horses also develop these patterns of life.

For example, foals' priorities are: to suck, follow the mother, sleep, play; fixed norms of behaviour that become more dynamic and flexible as they grow. This environmental scheme is influenced and modelled by learning and individual personality. Instinct is educated with training. Although sucking is also an instinctive action, the foal has to learn to do it in an efficient way and, since all animals are different, each one expresses their instinctive actions in their own particular way.

A nervous and skittish colt might want to flee if he is threatened by a man, while a frustrated or resentful horse might react by biting or attacking the person. But there are some norms of behaviour, such as the sexual one, that mature with age.

Circumstances, as well as how horses are raised, influence the way in which they classify environmental stimuli. A colleague told me the following story: "Not long ago, I treated a horse who got sick as soon as he was born. Local dogs, especially female dogs, took care of him as if he had been part of their pack. Now that the foal is healthy, he is friendly with dogs, but if they bother him, he scares them away. This group is accustomed to 'its dogs' but keeps 'strangers' away. A horse who has never had contact with a dog, might get scared as if the animal were a wolf. There are horses who are friendly with cats, sheep or other animals with whom they have shared their life as foals, so they have classified those stimuli as positive."

Evolution and adaptation

According to Darwin, the characteristics of the species have evolved by a process of natural selection caused by environmental pressure – ecological pressure – and sexual preferences. Behaviour development would be part of an evolutionary and adaptation process. During those processes, nervous mechanisms involved in responses to the environment have become more and more efficient. Features that favour reproductive success tend to increase in the population, while inefficient features tend to diminish it.

Chapter VI

These features include the psychological mechanisms that have a genetic component. The evolutionary process will be produced within the genetic code – cellular DNA – a process which Darwin denominated "evolution of features."

The animal psyche will be the result of a group of inherited neurological programmes. Instincts would be the product of the union between neurons and algorithms (small norms of behaviour) used to corroborate responses to the changing environment. Therefore, horse behaviour is not the direct and invariable result of instincts. Desires and aversions, motivations and elections would be produced by the information, transmitted by means of connections and electrophysical events inside the brain neuronal unions. So the mind is more than the mere sum of its parts because intangible thoughts can produce certain conduct. According to an English researcher, animals would "inherit" memories from positive experiences of their ancestors.

This process, which has a special purpose, was the result of the construction of thousands of algorithms in which the neuronal unions were developed in sequence with every new adaptation. The more powerful and comprehensive the system became, the more perfect its adaptation response to environment changes became. Genetics fed the nervous system and the algorithms so that horses would use them in their interaction with the environment. A herd, or an instinctive norm of behaviour, would be a unity of form or organisation, just like the atom. This unity is organised in hierarchies of units within units; like a structure that is repeated in every hierarchical social group.

Inside and around this unity, we would find a field that organises characteristic structures and activity patterns, designing the form and behaviour at every level of complexity. The term "field" includes fields of social and mental behaviour. They are formed and stabilised by a memory which is transmitted from generation to generation over the course of time, because fields would have a type of memory that tends to be more and more habitual. According to this hypothesis, conscious and unconscious brain activity would take place inside and through these morphic fields (R. Sheldrake), which contain a kind of in-built memory. Something like a group or species intelligence, that is superior to individual intelligence. That is the case of a flock of birds who fly as if they were one, for example.

As humans, we know very well that experience learning – trial and error – is quite hard, sometimes even frustrating, so these trials can be fatal for horses. On the contrary, instinctive responses are programmed responses, much faster, better directed and more reliable. In a way, and because of species intelligence, horses have the memory of what has been and what is dangerous now. In contrast to predators, prey animals are born complete, because it is vital for them to be able to follow their group if circumstances require it. A normal foal can stand up during the first half hour of life and that moment is one of fast learning because preys need to learn fast with the least waste of energy possible, and also need to communicate what they have learnt without delay. In the chapter about language, we described equines' subtle signalling system, as well as its purposes: to warn about a danger or the presence of food, to establish social hierarchy, to communicate their state of mind and, mainly, to keep the herd together. This signalling system has evolved during the process of formation of new neuronal connections that brought about efficient responses that allowed them to survive and adapt to different climate changes. But the communication process is much wider in terms of quality, variability and subtleness that is present in every gesture.

In conclusion, their norms of behaviour would be the result of evolutionary and adaptation processes in the nervous system, as well as memory and species intelligence that would be transmitted from generation to generation. Those are the features that proved to be efficient to guarantee the life of the group. The horse is an animal of habit who needs to live with calm and stability, that is why it is natural that a competition horse feels good. If habits are clear and the relationship with people that surround them is agreeable, the horse feels good. Useful decisions produce efficient responses towards the environment and these experiences are registered in neuronal events. These decisions depend on motivations, and it is during training that the horse is motivated with the idea of making his task agreeable. Basically, the horse needs clear leadership.

If you leave, I'd like to go with you.

Campero

In order to finish this chapter, let us look at the case of Campero, a horse who was anxious due to lack of clear leadership.

Chapter VI

Campero.

During a course in the equestrian center La Gerencia in Cantabria, northern Spain, I worked with this horse who won the reputation of being "bad" or "stupid." He was not easy to handle, walked out of the box in a hurry and when the horsewoman wanted to get him into the track, he reared. The workers also said he was not easy to handle.

The difficulty lay in the lack of leadership, and due to this lack, he was anxious and exited because he felt insecure.

Instability aroused in him the need for self protection, because others did not do it. How did he protect himself? In his own way: trying to walk out of the box in a hurry, running straight into others, rearing up so as not to enter the track. From his perspective, he was doing the right thing, because those attitudes were defensive. Nobody knew how to put limits on him, or how to make him feel secure; therefore, if there was no leader, somebody had to be, and so he himself would be.

The working steps were as follows:

First, I entered the box. I was told he was impetuous when you entered. Actually, he was full of energy and in need of communication. He could not use his force or communicate the way he needed; therefore, frustrated as he was, when someone entered the box he wanted to do everything at the same time, as is the horse's way. Make contact as soon as possible! Campero was a considerable size. Therefore, excited and in a hurry, it was difficult to work with him, so people logically got frightened. I began trying to communicate with him in his gesture language: when he came straight at me, I stimulated his chest so he moved back, or I made curt gestures with my arms, like a feline who is about to attack. He quickly understood that he could trust me and, at the same time, I signalled the equine codes. Which codes? The first was respect for the personal sphere. I did not allow him to invade me, I just stared at him or pushed him with my hands against his chest, and he quickly understood that he had to keep a distance.

The second step was to see how he got out of the box. Obviously, he did it in a hurry and quite disorderly. It was not his fault. It was natural, he was not working hard. So, when he could go out, he wanted to do it fast, and as they did not know how to handle him, he did what he could!!!

The second time we went out of the box, I did not allow him to do it in a hurry; just with a "friendly hand" – that is to say, a long riding crop with which I touched his chest so he felt uneasy if he tried to hurry – he understood that when he walked calmly behind me, without hurry, it felt good. On the contrary, if he was in a rush and came straight at me, he would feel a soft but unpleasant tap on his chest. The positive reinforcement involved releasing pressure, while the negative one, consisted in making him feel something agreeable simultaneously with the intention or action.

After entering 2 or 3 times, he understood what I wanted from him. This exercise was later performed by some students and he demonstrated how willing he was, because he entered and left the box very calmly with all the students. It is exactly the opposite of what people usually do, that is to say, shouting, mistreating the horse, beating him. Why are these methods, which imply punishment, violence, aggression or fear, not enough? Because the horse responds only out of fear; and a scared horse, just like a child or adult, does not have the possibility of "learning." He just tries to respond correctly so as to avoid punishment. We want the horse to learn and respond because he wants to, because he "knows" that if he does the right thing he does the best, and then he wants to do it. The horse calms down when he feels supported by a reliable person. He begins to "think" in his own terms - and that is what happened to Campero.

The third step was to take him to another place, where we gave him a massage. The massage let us enter the animal's body: investigate, perceive and observe his reactions, get to know him better. To see the way he behaves with others provides more elements to get to know him in depth. Although at the beginning he was alert to the external environment, which is logical, once he came into contact with us, he began to relax and started a body dialogue with the people from the course.

The only thing he needed was *communication*! Something we could offer with affection. The massage helped him relax and connect with his own body.

The following day, the fourth step consisted of repeating the exercises from the first day: to stay in the box without invading and coming in and out without hurry. As he responded with calm during the exercises, we took him for a ride in the club to see how he was haltered and how he behaved with other horses. He did well and, although he was in a bit of a hurry, he did it out of enthusiasm, not because he felt he needed to. We took him to a track that was quite muddy. This was the fifth step. He worked great with me and then with one of the attendees of the course with whom he got on very well from the beginning. This man transmitted calm to him and the horse received that feeling with great pleasure. We worked the body posture of this person so the horse could understand what he was being asked to. That is how we managed to soften him on both sides and we left him "thinking" when he stretched his body and relaxed the head.

We let him loose and he chose to stay at the nearest corner from the place where there was movement of people and horses. He took advantage of the strokes from the people who passed by, some of whom where really surprised to see him so relaxed.

In the afternoon, we took step six, which consisted of coming into and out of the track. Although they had told me the problem would arise when he had to enter mounted, I wanted to observe how he behaved when he came into and out of the track without anyone mounting him. He looked calm, he did not show any difficulties.

The third day, I decided to mount him to test his reaction. He was certainly a little reluctant to enter the track, but with a firm impulse, without letting him "think", he finally entered. After working for a while, the last step consisted of repeating the action several times. In a moment, before he entered the track he reared and, at the same time, I responded with a high tone of voice, just a touch with the riding crop and a firm impulse with the legs moving him forward, a moment in which he relaxed and entered without difficulties. The problem was that the person who mounted him did not know how to handle him, so Campero learnt that if he reared, he could dominate the situation, so they did not mount him. Horses always try to save energy; in this case, due to lack of leadership, Campero was not motivated by his horsewoman and had no interest in entering the track. If the person does not know how to handle the horse properly, he will behave exactly like him in different ways.

Some people say that the horse takes advantage of the situation, which is half true. Actually, the animal looks for a situation in which he feels safe and motivated, a situation that, to a certain extent, reminds him of his life in the herd. If he does not feel comfortable when he is being mounted, because of lack or excess of leadership, the horse will feel "insecure", "anxious", "worried", because something is wrong. In human terms, he takes advantage of the situation, but in equine terms, his reaction is perfectly normal.

CHAPTER VII

COMMUNICATION

Cossack with Girl (Radionov – 1994)

We are going for a ride, my horse.
The Great Father wants us to ride easy,
not to run over anyone.
Thus, we will go fine my little horse.
We will go to a meeting
and you will ride, your eyes looking up.
My dear little horse.
Let us have good luck at the meeting.
Let us go and come back well.
And thus you shall be a good horse.

Ulcantum[1] to be chanted when riding a horse

DON HILARIO AIGO - MAPUCHE

We are going for a ride with my horse.

The most important aspect in the relationship with horses is, as with humans, communication.

What is *communication*? As we have already mentioned, it is the action and the result of communicating something or communicating between beings. The bond established between certain things, the relationship between people, implies fluid communication. Some synonyms are: message, correspondence, connection, treatment, transmission, relationship, exchange. Therefore, communication is a dynamic process of information exchange, in which two or more individuals participate. It is not a unilateral or dictatorial process.

For many people the corporal, silent language of horses is difficult to understand. Perhaps it is because their auditory or visual capacity is more developed, whereas their body perception is less developed, something that hinders their capacity for understanding a communication system based on corporal, silent signals. They are the kind of people who need to "see in order to believe", or need to hear and listen to words. Therefore, it is logical that they find it difficult to understand the silence of horses or see their signals.

Several research programmes and current experiences with different animals, such as dolphins, whales and elephants among others, are demonstrating the existence of a world that was largely ignored and hardly understood. A lot of people now work

---

[1] Chanted poetry or praise, of Mapuche origin

Chapter VII

with animals in assisted therapies due to the ability they have to communicate with children, and due to the positive effects they have on them.

Therefore, getting acquainted with this type of experience is and will be positive: for animals, for the children who become connected with them and for adults interested in knowing them better.

The first step in learning to communicate with horses is to *respect and listen to them*. A few years ago, a horsewoman told me this anecdote: "I was working with my mare in a big pasture when some friends who were outside started calling me. When I tried to approach them, my mare stopped and refused to move on. Since I was surprised by her attitude, which was not normal, I tried to make her move, but did not succeed. So I decided to work in circles with her, when one of my friends shouted: 'There is a snake!' We were all astonished since we had never seen a snake in that place before." Apparently, many times horses have things to tell us.

In this communication process, both parties end up winning. Men learn a way of being silent; learn to perceive things, to listen, to ask themselves questions and to lead without cruelty, peacefully and consistently. The horse develops his sensory and motor systems, his intelligence becomes sharper and he is able to use his tools more efficiently.

At this point, I would like to transcribe some paragraphs from a lecture given in 1971 at the Institute of Cultural Research, London, by the English investigator into animal behaviour, Edward Campbell: "Knights in the Middle Ages, engaged in combats of chivalry, developed certain tricks in their charges. A horse would be trained to lash out with hind hooves at a certain moment and so secure the knight's back. Or it would rear up, swing round and paw the air, so as to discourage an opponent engaging from the front. With the end of knightly combat the functional aspect of this vanished, but the horse movements seem to have become stylised and elaborated as 'Haute Ecole' riding. In the last century the centre of this fine-art horse-training was the Spanische Reitschule at Vienna, associated with the flourishing days of the Austro-Hungarian Empire. There, high school riding reached very high standards of refinement, but there were other places where the same – or perhaps even a superior – standard was achieved.

Therese Renz, a member of a famous European circus dynasty, seems to have taken school riding to an exceptional pitch. She was still riding when she was over 80 and could produce even then a remarkable effect on audiences. A German publicist, Dr Kober made some interesting observations. In brief, the theory is that at a certain pitch of high school training and at a certain degree of rapport between horse and rider, 'something else' switches in. The brain of the horse goes into abeyance and the rider's brain takes charge of two motor-instinctive circuits – the horse's and the rider's own.

Dr Kober noticed that when this 'something' happened it was communicated instantly to an audience, whether it was an audience of farmers in Bavaria or to a sophisticated society audience in Berlin. The phenomenon communicated itself. People felt they were in the presence of something in an unfamiliar area and, though they could not rationalise it, they could not fail to notice it.

Is it possible that something of man's intelligence can be imparted by some sort of emanation as the result of long association?

Man and animal have been associated almost from the start of human evolution. There appears to have been both a magic and a domestic relationship. Maybe the two lines sometimes overlap. Could it be that the man-animal relationship is one of reciprocal advantage at some level that is not easily seen? That man – though unconsciously – is contributing something to an animal's evolution? Some of the suggestions I have made are no doubt fanciful and they have to be labelled with a very big question mark."

MALENKI AND JADRIFT. UNUSUAL COMMUNICATION PHENOMENA

When I was a little girl, I had a jumping horse, Malenki - 15 years old, a beautiful sabino gray who came from a regiment. He was a "serious" horse, and was not used to being carefully treated. Due to his manner of being serious and not very expressive, at first I had trouble connecting with him. I was used to playing with horses and he did not know how to play.

Yet, he was my "master horse", since he was very good at jumping, and was determined and self-confident. Many times, I made mistakes and he avoided knocking down some hurdles, such as when I entered out of distance or when I did not loose the reins enough at the necessary distance. As time went by, he got used to being treated differently, and we succeeded in making a good binomial. He spent some time at a barracks, in Buenos Aires. There, I took him out for a ride through the nearby woods. In those days, people participated in politics at certain establishments where they would

This mare has just played polo. Her face is pure expression; her senses sharp; her mind open. How many messages is she transmitting that we still do not understand?

Chapter VII

also play music. One day, when we were passing near one of those places, they were playing some march and, as soon as Malenki heard it, he started dancing! It was very funny because the people there came out to applaud him. I was surprised; I had no idea he could be so precise in following the rhythm and the time. Then I got used to it, and every time we won prizes at jumping competitions, I let him dance as he pleased.

One day, while we were going to a riding club to take part in a competition, he had a very painful incident in the middle of a road. Suddenly, at a rail barrier, I realised he had difficulties in walking, and he was sweating white foam all over his body. I was alone; at first I got desperate, but then I managed to calm down. I did not know what was happening to him until afterwards; the only thing I could think of was singing and talking to him, telling him to hang on, that we would arrive soon, and he slowly started walking and we managed to get to the club. The diagnosis was renal colic. The veterinarians who saw him could not believe he could have walked in the condition he was in. They attended him and we came back in a trailer. When he was feeling really bad, he completely gave in to me and we managed to get there. Some time later, when I returned from my holidays, I found him with a very deep wound on his back right leg, at the level of the hock (tarsus). So, in order to treat him daily, I took him to a field near my house. But something weird happened, which kept me thinking for a long time. One day I went to see him before a class but did not come very near him, as I usually did. I did not know why. I left, with a strange feeling. Fifteen hours later, I was taking a yoga class and started having tachycardia, for the first time in my life.

Then I went to study at a friend's house. In the evening, I was told my parents would pick me up, which surprised me, since I was supposed to go back by bus. I thought it was because of an argument I had had with my mother that morning. When they came to pick me up, I got into the car and my mother told me: "We need to tell you something, Anahí". I answered: "I know, Malenki died". My mother, shocked, asked me: "How did you know?" I answered: "I don't know, but I just knew". This episode, apart from being very sad and shocking for me, made me understand how many communication levels exist with animals.

This was not the only time something like that happened to me. Another experience occurred on a Wednesday evening in 1997. I was at home, studying, when suddenly I felt a deep urge to go to the Palermo racetrack stud, where I had many horses under my care. I did not know why, but I followed my feelings. When I got there, I heard some painful neighs, inside a locked box. Since the stud workers were not there, because they had gone to run to La Plata, I looked for the place where the neighs came from, until I reached the box of the mare Jadrift. The labourer from the stud right next to it helped me open the box door. The mare was lying down, distressed and moaning. She stood up, scratched her tail, and looked at her right side. She was in deep pain. While

Communication

Synchrony: field of action of two binomials.

I went home to look for the medication, the labourer made her walk, a manoeuvre usually recommended when horses suffer from colic. I came back 30 minutes later, gave her a homeopathic medication and, 5 minutes later, she defaecated, and 10 minutes later she urinated and calmed down. It was a mild to moderate colic, but a very painful and dangerous one. Many horses die due to colic if they are not treated immediately.

Some people and some researchers claim that horses communicate through telepathy. They say the animal has a map of the people and animals who are part of their life. Apparently, this form of communication would be possible thanks to simple thoughts, words, feelings, smells and images to and from the animal and, of course, between people. But, since we are neither used to nor trained in this subtler kind of communication, we usually reject it out of ignorance. But the fact that it is rejected does not mean it does not occur.

These events are not esoteric; they are part of a communication ability that truly exists, even though traditional science denies its existence, or even though, due to lack of training, it is not usually studied. Somehow, in order to understand what had happened, I had to study and find reference in research carried out by scientists who accept these facts and study them in depth. Therefore, I focus the study of communication on the premise that, among beings organised in societies, there would exist a common field which causes them to be connected by a higher form of thought and communication capacity. This concept, referred to by the Harvard biochemist Rupert Sheldrake as "morphic fields", was first introduced by investigations into certain features of animal behaviour, such as sense of direction, telepathy and premonition, and for which traditional science has no explanation from a mechanistic biological perspective.

I believe that communication with animals allows us to have access to a very subtle aspect of communication, and it is useful, not only with animals, but also with people. From my experience as a veterinarian, understanding the meaning of horses' silent signals and signs poses a great challenge for me, in the sense that I cannot take anything for granted; thus, it encourages me to investigate in other fields. Quantum physics and other dynamic and vitalistic sciences conceive these processes as part of a permanent greater evolutionary process of the planet. According to modern cosmology, the entire universe is in a permanent state of evolution, like a progressive transformation, with purpose and intent.

Ancient physicians and philosophers did not break man or nature into pieces in order to study them; their aim as doctors was to cure body and mind; for them, curing was not limited to treating the physical disease, it had a transcendental sense aimed at people's lives, that is, at making life useful in every possible way.

To cure meant that people could use their tools to their full potential. These doctors and philosophers suggested a concept of union between all beings. Their approach was vitalistic, it stated that everything in nature has a transcendental sense: intention, purpose. A rose's seed carries the information that it will become a rose. When a mare gets pregnant, she will only foal a filly or a colt, not a dog, because every being has a purpose, everything works with an intention. The horse has the intention of "being a horse." "You shall be what you have to be, or you shall be nothing at all", General José de San Martín said.

From this perspective, nature would be something dynamic, neither mechanical nor static. As if there was a creative power operating in the physical world and causing the phenomena that occurs inside it, like a combination of essential qualities that belong to each being, with their main characteristics. It is a life force, an impulse by which the activities of living organisms are produced. From the standpoint of conventional science, nature is made of matter, fields and energy, and is governed by the laws of nature, studied in depth by the Greeks. Cosmos means "beautiful order" and the Greeks studied that order so as to understand its laws.

Aristotle stated that the principle of life can be identified with: spirit, soul, self being and psyche. Later on, St Thomas Aquinas completed that statement. In his study on psyche, he proposed a model of man, understood as a substantial compound of soul and body, a man with a transcendental sense, of noble origin, whose aim in the world is to know and act in a correct way. This way of studying man and the world states that there is a formative cause and a final cause or purpose in all living beings. There is always a purpose in life, which brings about the evolution of behaviour and of harmonic mental processes. Therefore, according to supporters of vitalism, living organisms are truly alive and have intentions and purposes. On the contrary, the Cartesian standpoint is not functional for this study, since it states that systems are inanimate and essentially mechanical.

Morphic fields

The morphic unit is a form or organisation unit, like a cell, an animal, an instinctive behaviour pattern, or a social group. These units are organised in hierarchies of units inside units: for example, a crystal has molecules, which in turn has atoms, which in turn has electrons, and so on. The morphic field would be an area of physical influence, which relates matter to energy in its domain of influence. In ordinary physics there are different types of fields, such as the gravitational or electromagnetic fields. This morphic field would be located inside and around a unit which organises its characteristic structure and its activity pattern; its function is to strengthen the form and behaviour of morphic units at all levels of complexity. ***This hypothesis of the formative cause predicts that: when an animal of a given species learns a new pattern of behaviour, other animals of the same species, all around the world, tend to learn the same pattern, faster, due to a process of resonance.*** The more they learn, the easier learning will be for others. Through this resonance, formative influence travels in time and space, since it is an influence that comes from the past. The higher the influence of the morphic resonance, the higher the degree of similarity. Units that were very similar in the past are subject to resonating from their past. Some sort of "living" memory.

In self-organised systems, like the groups in which social animals live, the morphic field helps keeping them together and coordinating their activity. Sheldrake states that animals respond to a collective field, like a higher intelligence, which also occurs in shoals of fish, packs of wolves and human groups. Sometimes, we can see how huge herds of horses move together in a general and very fluid movement, without colliding, each one moving in a unique way. As if they did it "without" thinking. Every animal who moves in a group has to do it in a very precise way so as not collide with another one; each one has to deeply trust the rest of them.

A good example of how these fields work is that of someone who avoids an accident when driving his car; if you ask him "How did you avoid crashing?", he will answer "I didn't think about it!"; it is like having the ability of sensing what other motorists do right or wrong. The only possible explanation is that there is a higher and subtler communication level, something telepathic. This means that groups of social animals, the same as humans, would be coordinated by these fields. When a horse or another animal meets a human being, this field is created. Usually, this relationship is called "social bond", but "bond" is just a word, a metaphor, whereas the morphic field is a real connection.

These concepts allow us to understand the reasons why, when the owner of a horse goes far away, the bond between them remains and acts as a subtler communication channel. Although some people do not believe that this bond works at a distance, others have had experiences that confirm it, for example, a mother who feels that her son is not well and gets a call from school to tell her that he has a fever and she has to pick him up. Those fields have measurable effects, but the core of this concept is that it relates these animals' phenomena with a broader theory about social behaviour and with an even broader conceptualisation about self-organised systems in general, not only social groups.

Animals keep us in touch with our instincts. The contact with them stimulates us and helps us to know and look after nature. Sheldrake says: "The bond with non-human nature is absolutely essential; strictly speaking, a part of our own human nature requires maintaining that connection. The comprehension and study of these telepathic bonds with animals will help us reconnect with the animal kingdom, or at least recognise more explicitly that this bond does exist."

Laboratory scientists who experiment with animals do not establish emotional bonds. On the contrary, owners of pets and other animals share daily life with them, something that enables them to get to know the subtleties of communication and their lives. We, as humans, also have our own animal faculty, so we share some behaviours with our "little brothers", as Saint Francis of Assisi called them.

The artificial conditions set by some scientists to investigate animal behaviour seem to have been designed for proving how different they are from us, or that the differences are the result of lack of intelligence; they neither take into account the animals' real abilities, nor their ecological niche, the tools which they count on, or the precise function for which they have been created.

Dogs are prepared to discover and pry into the world through their smell; therefore, saying they are useless because they do not use their hands is a sign of lack of intelligence from the researcher.

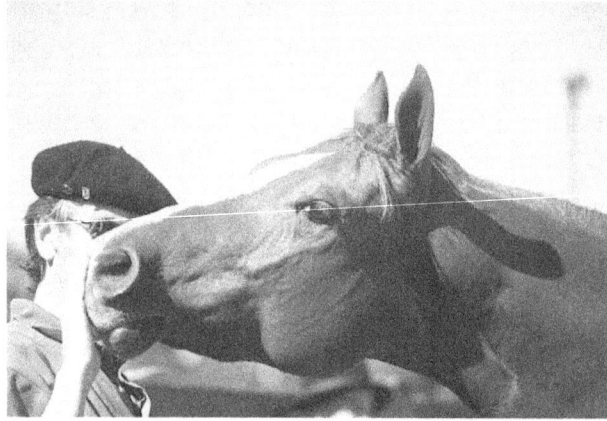

Men and animals have been related since the beginning of human evolution. The possibility of a balanced relationship is part of human and animal nature. We should discover and get to know that capacity in order to fully develop it. The development of that capacity probably influences our evolution as a species and the evolution of animals in a positive way.

Pictures 39, 40 and 41
Synchrony of these binomials and of the group.

Picture 42: A herd in the morphic field.

Picture 43: A foal who has never been touched with the intention of getting to know the person.

Picture 44: Personality.

Anticipation, intuition or telepathic prediction abilities are not different from the ability to flee at a great speed or jump high. Talent for premonition is an ability that the horse has developed in order to survive; therefore, the favoured ones will be those animals that can anticipate danger and those who have the capacity for self-organisation, because they will have a great advantage over those who hurt themselves when they run at great speed, or over those who have difficulties in accepting the coexistence of social rules.

If horses are capable of communicating at such a subtle level, and chimpanzees are capable of expressing deep grief or anguish (as Jane Goodall has demonstrated), we cannot keep treating animals as if they are objects, because they are not toys to be used as we please, like those dogs some people buy during holidays and then abandon or leave at the side of the road, or racing horses who are left in the countryside or sent to the slaughterhouse because they did not get a prize. The planet is a living organism. Obviously, we have not been functioning properly lately.

Synchrony

This refers to an event that occurs outside time and space, in another dimension as a more elevated operation of human conscience.

Rupert Sheldrake describes a striking phenomenon called "Bacteria feelings": "Quorum sensing." There are some fishes that emit light because they have small bags in their abdominal region that are practically full of bacteria that produce light.

These bacteria were cultivated but did not produce light at first. While scientists wondered what was missing in the cultural medium, bacteria continued to grow and generated such a rich and abundant medium that one day they began to produce light. What happened? They needed a certain density of population, a quorum to begin creating light. This mystery that seemed quite surprising at the beginning was then clarified when they realised every bacterium emitted a certain substance that was, in turn, transmitted to another bacterium that was close to it, and so on, so they became full of that substance and when they reached a given concentration, they told the genetic system to start generating the other enzymatic system to produce light.

We are in the presence of a resonance effect, a cooperation effect, *synergos*, in Greek terms, a joint work. This synchrony might be observed, for example, in important historical binomials: Alexander and Bucephalus, El Cid and Babieca and our 19th century *caudillo*[2] from La Rioja province, Facundo Quiroga with his horse Piojo, called Moro due to his coat.

---

[2] Spanish word for "leader"

Chapter VII

> Facundo Quiroga had a close relationship with his horse. According to his wife, Dolores, Moro was Facundo's oracle, because he believed his horse had supernatural powers and he followed his advice. The *caudillo* preferred to stay in the country to take care of the horse instead of going to the city and be honoured, and he slept under an awning near the animal.
>
> *As a wizard,*
> *His fellow countrymen thought*
> *Again mounting his horse*
> *Making the plains shake*
>
> According to the story, the day of the decisive battle, Moro did not want to be mounted. Despite the warning, Facundo decided to fight. It was a terrible loss, because his horse Moro was captured by the enemy, and he could never recover the horse.
>
> One of Quiroga's officers told the other officers who mocked at the horse: "I witnessed the moment in which the General tried to mount him the day of the battle and the horse did not allow us to bridle him, no matter the efforts, being I one of the men who tried to do it, and just to manifest the annoyance he felt for the disdain with which the General responded to his warnings."
>
> Facundo felt invulnerable with his horse, whose loss caused him a great sorrow, even health problems. He was never the same…

These thinking patterns, that regard the universe as a dynamic design that is in permanent change, allow us to understand how a gregarious animal, like the horse, can be mentally organised to live in a group, and how the same group organises itself to act as such. Horses and other animals do not simply function like a mechanism of action and reaction. Racing horses transmit to their descendants the ability to run, in the same way that dressage horses transmit their capacity to dance. This fact, that used to be explained from a genetic point of view, would be influenced by collective memory, and the individual experience could make contribution to that memory. Therefore, we have to see the world beyond the ways that we are accustomed to.

Intention

The word "intention" comes from the Latin verb *intendo*, which means: to indicate, to signal. Animal behaviour expresses intention, which is easily observed due to the versatile responses when they confront certain challenges, like a filly who stole a carrot and beat it against a post to cut it. Animals have perceptions, express emotions, solve problems and have memory. Some researchers say that animal cognition might be unconscious; however, some others investigate the idea that many animals, from insects to birds, have a very precise knowledge of some aspects of their environment and their society. These researchers recognise that certain internal cognitive processes like learning and memory, problem solving, concept formation and intention, have important effects upon animal behaviour. Thus, denying the existence of conscience in every animal, with the exception of the human being, is an obstacle to knowledge. Why do we have to accept the idea that animals spend their lives like unconscious "somnambulists" arguing that their mental processes are not accessible to scientific analysis?

Probably, when animals communicate between themselves they are informing simple conscious thoughts and emotional feelings. According to cognitive ethologists, animal communication is complete and sufficient to communicate simple thoughts.

Mental processes can be deduced and induced by means of a scientific and objective analysis of behaviour. Through intention, animals can optimise their integration with the environment stimuli using their appetites: desires, aversions, sensations, joy, sorrow, anger and fear.

Different cognitive states

According to Dr. Marthe Kiley-Worthington, horses can learn a vocabulary of about 300 words. She has been investigating for more than five years with a test that can measure the potential for language learning. Her horses are capable of learning nouns, verbs and adjectives such as "soft" or "strong." They also show signs of understanding emotional terms such as "fear" and "joy." The method of study is the following: horses are kept in groups and begin training from birth. They take 15 minutes "classes" a week with people who "help them learn." They are taught the words that correspond to objects like "buckets" or "blankets." In order to learn words that describe actions, people pronounce the word at the same time they perform the action. Then, they stop making the gesture so the horse responds to the word. Later, horses go to "structured expeditions" in which people talk about what the horse or person is doing, for example: "Shemal (the horse) eats grass." Or "Jane (the person) is on the phone."

Worthington proved that her students can select blue, red or yellow buckets just with a verbal sign, and they can perform activities such as kicking a ball or picking up a blanket when they are asked to. Besides, she says that her animals seem to react to words such as "frightened" and that: "One of my horses yawns if I ask him to. Another one stops putting his nose on the ground when he is told that it pricks, no matter if he is about to eat pricks." Her horses react to words – she does not use gestures – they learn to listen to the words and understand the meaning. She uses the same technique used in evolutionary psychology with children that have not started to talk.

Evidently, due to their physiology, horses do not learn to speak the way humans do; nonetheless, this study shows that they have an ability to comprehend which is greater than we thought.

Personality and identity

In this context, with these dynamic ideas in mind, let us see if horses have personality. What is personality? It is the individual difference that constitutes every person and distinguishes it from another. It is the collection of characteristics or original qualities that stand out in some people, qualities that constitute the person or intelligent subject. In Latin, "person" means actor's mask, a theatre character. In the past, it meant a character in a play. "Person" is a word that refers to a unique individual different from any other, being recognised as unique because of its mental and behavioural characteristics. Given these definitions, it is strange to find people connected to horses that deny the fact that they have personality, especially those who have spent most of their lives with them.

The personality of each horse or human being reflects the sum of their genetic heritage and their life experience; and at the same time it is more than that, it is an intangible and indefinable quality that makes an individual unique. Every horse is more than the sum of his parts.

Now, how do horses recognise their individuality? They leave odoriferous messages, the equine equivalent for "Charles was here." So we might suppose that leaving messages that identify ourselves implies that we have a sense of identity.

When my mare sees me coming, she knows that I will probably take her somewhere else, so most of the times she urinates or defaecates where she is, to leave her mark: "Jadrift was here." Other times she shows me something, she looks at some horse or place she wants me to look at. I also observe this fact in a group of sister mares that live with their mother. They live loose and when I arrive they welcome me and if I look for one of them to mount, before leaving, as soon as they see me, they defaecate or urinate in the last place where they were. Maybe there is something subtler in those actions that I cannot fully understand.

Many people who are in daily contact with horses accept and find it obvious that they have a sense of identity. According to some cognitive psychologists, animals and very little children do not think of themselves in the first person singular. For example, a 2 year-old girl, named Caroline, does not say "I love George", she says "Caroline loves George" instead, because her name is her personal identification. It is interesting to note that some sportsmen and politicians speak in third person to refer to themselves when they are interviewed. Apparently, horses identify themselves with the names they were given or the name used in relation to them. The name becomes the first person for the animal.

Dr. Donald Griffin, professor at Rockefeller University, and a pioneer in the study of animal cognition, believes animals might have names for each other, although these would not be expressed in words, of course. In fact, words are not always necessary, even for advanced conceptual thinking. Odoriferous marks might be considered a form of "signature" and it is possible that horses might be able to think in images. Some research has been carried out in which the mare listens to her foal neigh and she recognises him perfectly.

When the owners of the horses meet them, they greet them with their name and many respond with a neigh. In the sisters' herd, each one responds to her name when they are called, by raising the ears, neighing or coming closer. It is evident that they recognise their names.

In his book *My Horses, My Teachers*, Colonel Alois Podhajsky, director of the Spanish Riding School in Vienna, remembers the great Nero with whom he won a bronze medal in the 1936 Olympics. He says that after being abroad for a while, he went to see Nero as he used to do every time he came back from a trip. But, while he was abroad, Nero was stabled with sick horses, with another 40 horses, and he could not find him in the dark. "Frustrated and sad, I was about to leave, when as a last try I called him by his pet name, Burschi, and Nero immediately responded whispering from the farthest corner of the stable."

Horses recognise and remember their old friends: horses, people, other animals, although they have not seen them for ages. Podhjasky had to train a mare called Judith, who was not easy, according to the owner, but with whom he had no problem to empathise. Unfortunately, when he was advanced in the training, the owner decided to sell her and Podhjasky did not see her until a year later during a show. He describes what happened when the owner showed him the mare: "She was indifferent inside the box, without paying attention. I called her by the pet name used with her. As long as I live, I will never forget how she raised her head and put her ears straight as if she was looking for the owner of that voice in her memory. Slowly, she turned around, came towards us and greeted me with a soft neigh, rubbing her nose against my shoulder in a familiar gesture. His owner was surprised and murmured: "That's funny; this strange creature never comes to me. I can call her and call her but she won't come…" This story is quite significant. Gnomo also had quite a noticeable expression of recognition after a long time without seeing us. An acquaintance bought him and told me he would be in a club near my house. It had been more than a year since I last saw him. When I got to

Chapter VII

the adjoining park, I saw him tied to a tree and called him. It was a touching response, he turned around with his ears pointing at me and he reared. When I got closer, quite excited to see him, I said: "It's OK Gnomo, stay calm", and he immediately relaxed and I could stroke him calmly.

Now it is worth asking: Is it possible that they do not want to remember certain people while they do want to remember others? Every horse needs a different form of contact and communication. A friend's mare needs to "argue and quarrel a little", as if she did not want to be subjugated. Although she is not mean, she needs to be "respected." It is that simple. Because when he mounts her, she is completely docile and attentive to what you ask her. But these are her characteristics. It is useful to have an idea of how the animal is, but the best way to know him is through contact. Just as we understand a person once we make contact with him/her, the same happens with a horse.

CHAPTER VIII

WHAT CAN WE LEARN FROM THE MOST INTELLIGENT HORSES?

CASE I
MONTE, A RACING HORSE

Buddha on a flying horse (Korean art)

The day he started rehabilitation.

In my professional experience and through exchanges with colleagues and people associated with horses, I have learned that many "problem" horses, in general, are more intelligent and sensitive than average horses. These horses have a bad reputation because they have difficulties in adapting and they are not easily handled or understood. But from my point of view, they are the most interesting ones, in the sense that they pose new questions because they represent a challenge for investigation and learning. In this first practical case we will analyse Monte, a racing horse, son of Mountdrago, who stopped running at the age of five because he did not want to cross the starting gate.

Let us take a look at his story.

He was my patient during two periods of his life. The first, when he was weaned and the owner took him to the country in Luján, in the Buenos Aires province. Then he was a lively and tame foal, but he had quite a defined personality. He was characterised by being quite an independent foal and, although he was part of a group of foals recently weaned, he "cut loose", he stayed near the group without being dependent. The labourer who took care of him said he was the first he would call to eat in the morning and was the only one who jumped the wire fence to the other paddock in order to get food.

He did not seem to be the leader of the group, because he got along very well with the others, although he maintained this individuality feature. Another feature I found striking was that, when he was enclosed in the box at night, on one occasion the

Chapter VIII

labourer scolded him for something he had done and, the following morning, when he entered the box to let him out, the horse was in a corner and had not eaten the food from the previous night. According to the labourer, the foal was offended, a feature of his personality I saw when he was an adult.

I stopped seeing him for two years, but I knew he was tamed by a person who works without violence, and when I saw him again, they told me the mounted horse was light and easy to work with, which I confirmed when I mounted him. He had a soft mouth, he behaved himself properly, was obedient and easy to handle.

The second time, when the owner asked me to treat the animal again, the horse had already worked with many people and I found him quite stressed due to his life at the stud. He had won two races at San Isidro Racetrack. He was no longer that trustful, affectionate, tame horse I had met before. He was in good shape, but he bit because he was frustrated and excited due to lack of social contact and communication, eventually, he had become an animal difficult to handle. The last groom told me that the last time they had tried to infiltrate him at the hocks, it was impossible to do because he kicked them constantly. They sent him to another stud, where he was very well treated, but he could not recover. He suffered from a right sacroiliac subluxation, so I advised the owner to send him to the country to rest for a few months so he could recover, but the owner preferred to continue with the infiltrations and other complementary treatments. Five more months were lost, because during the two races he ran at that time, although he crossed the starting gate correctly, he had problems with the initial jump, he feared pain and could not respond to the physical demands a race requires.

Finally, after these failures, the owner accepted that the horse should have the deserved and really necessary rest. He was sent to a cattle ranch where we began with physical and psychological rehabilitation work.

As a first measure, we rode him through the paddock to make him see the place and the wire fence, to prevent him from running out foolishly and getting killed.

After this work, we released him with another four geldings. Why? Because the horse, especially the stallion, is perfectly equipped at a psychological level to communicate with other members of the herd. Loneliness is the worst suffering for a horse. In the herd, stallions are always paying attention to their mares, they communicate with them, with their foals, with the colts and the fillies. They have quite an active life. When they do not, and do not receive anything in return, they get so frustrated that some of them end up biting others because they cannot express the physiological need of activity and communication. Frustration increases until they develop stereotypes to compensate for their unmet needs. It is essential for them to make olfactory, tactile, audible and visual contact with the others, because that is part of their nature and their survival needs. This

> *Loneliness is the worst suffering for a horse*

communication need is as important as it is to us.

The result was that Monte could socialise with these geldings, who quickly set him in his place and no one got hurt; on the contrary, the racing horse found himself thinking and acting as a horse. Together with this process of socialisation, I treated him with homeopathic medication and trace elements and I performed a permanent work with therapeutic massages and physical rehabilitation.

Monte learning to be a horse.

Later, he was transferred to another place where there was a round pen. This type of pen is adequate to perform body, visual and vocal communication exercises, positively reinforcing the animal when he does something right and pointing out what is wrong. In this case, Monte had to stop biting, had to let them shoe him and had to accept being handled easily. By means of "equine" gestures and signals, we managed to put him in the "human herd." He learned that, when he bit, he would get something unpleasant, but when he stopped doing it, he would get a reward.

If he was loose and wanted to bite, the most unpleasant thing for him was to make him walk or make sharp movements with my arms; if he was tied, I shook the halter. He kept thinking about the results of his actions because that is the way they learn in nature; I did not make him afraid, but I worked with his mind by means of an "operative conditioning." He had to earn that positive reinforcement; when he stopped biting, I released pressure, for example, I loosed the halter, I kept him still or I let him eat grass. The reward, the lack of it, or the negative reinforcement, like shaking the halter when he was biting, were simultaneous or immediately subsequent to the action. This process was repeated until he understood because it was easier to educate than to reeducate. Depending on the behavior disorder, and according to the horse, the process is easier or more difficult, but it is possible, and that is essential. Due to his learning ability, the horse can incorporate new information as well as he is capable of relearning and retaining.

Daniel, the owner of the place, is an excellent horse breaker and rider of Arab horses, a natural leader for them. Monte felt at ease with him, something that helped to regain his trust in men. The bond was so solid that they used to play, for example, when Daniel wet the sand at the pen, Monte placed himself behind him, trying to get wet.

Chapter VIII

Monte smelling his friend Martina.

I complemented this reeducation work, mounting him, flexing him and trying something different from traditional training. What for? In order to stimulate him to learn to use his body, his muscles and his motor skills to the full. The horse needs to use his entire body. Life in captivity makes him tense, his muscles tighten and he hurts himself, provoking a decrease in his body awareness.

A different training to the one he is accustomed to is also a good stimulus; therefore, I used that pause in his life to get him in touch with other possibilities for his body and mind. He responded so well that we were impressed. There is so much prejudice with racing horses that, when one works to dispel the myths, it is wonderful to see how capable they really are. This horse quickly demonstrated that he was able to begin with a new task such as training.

> *Any type of work that broadens the animal's conscience will be beneficial and useful to maximise his motor capacity.*

A month and a half since we began this rehabilitation work, he was so calm that it was difficult to believe that he was the same animal that used to bite and was not easy to handle. Several people had told me: "Be careful with this horse, he might kill you some day." I did not give them credit because I firmly believe that when there are problems with an animal, the problem is the people and not the animal.

He came back to the racetrack after three months of treatment with a groom who took up training again, respecting his time. A month later, together with a colleague, we gave him some mild and effective medicine, but we decided to avoid corticosteroids because this horse was too weak at the croup to tolerate such medicine. He responded quite well to the treatment, he came in and out of the starting gate normally, and we put him down to reprise as soon as he was in good shape. People at the stud could not believe he had been a "bad" animal. He behaved quite well and he had a labourer to whom he adapted really quickly. It is very important for the labourer to be careful, responsible and respectful because he is the person who spends most of the time with the animal and influences his mood and stability.

The resumption day arrived, and what happened left us astonished. The horse was calm and in good shape, without any pain, but when the starting gates opened, he stood still. He had entered normally, but when the gate opened, he moved back a little and stayed literally paralysed. After listening to what the jockey, the groom and the labourer said about him and, in order to understand what had happened, I inquired whether he had shown that behavior before I started to treat him, because the owner had not told me anything regarding that. The following day, comments were: "He is a smart horse because he knows how to differentiate the racing day from the practice day." Apparently, that was the case because that day he came in and out normally, and the same happened during the week.

Finally, the owner confessed that in La Plata city, the horse had shown that paralysing behavior at the starting gates and they solved it in the most unbelievable and cruel way: They obliged him to come out with barbed wires at the croup!

From these experiences, I cannot but wonder: What would happen to these individuals who have such intelligent minds if they were treated like that? How would they feel?

And here is the heart of the matter. The horse recovered physically and mentally. When he was treated with patience and respect, he found his abilities and intelligence again. And horses, just like us, remember the beneficial facts, the negative and the destructive ones. So, the question that arose was: What was the real motivation Monte needed to run again? What could humans give him so he would feel willing to run? I am sure that with the passing of time and motivating him with intelligence, he would have gone back to the tracks, but the owner had made a decision and did not give him enough time to recover.

The essence of this episode is that it is not fair to take advantage of the goodwill of horses to give what they have without respecting them as they deserve. They do not forget, and the better they are treated, the more they will give. The fact that they are winners or not does not depend on them, it depends on a variety of factors that are not their responsibility.

The experience with children with exceptional needs shows how positive they might become. The injustices are indignant, the abuses and mistreatment to which they are exposed by some people who call themselves men.

This story expresses, in brief, the aim of this chapter.

I saw a boy coming towards me with a sheep running after him.

'No wonder the sheep follows you so closely,' I remarked, 'attached to you as it is by that rope round its neck.

'The boy laughed and released the animal. Off it went, gamboling in delight. Then the boy made to move on. Immediately the sheep came to his heel and followed close behind. The youth smiled and gave it some barley.

'You were right, wise man,' he said, 'but as you see, the name of the rope is kindness.'

CHAPTER IX

CASE II
A TERRIFIED LITTLE HORSE

Arabs Chasing a Loose Arab Horse in an Eastern Landscape (John Frederick Herring I, 19th C)

Here, I am trying to rebuild the horse's sequences of communication

This is the case of a horse named Negrito, a Lusitano and English thoroughbred cross.

It is the jet black one in the picture, whom I was lucky enough to work with during a course at the Sierra Norte Equestrian Center in Spain. Before getting there, he had been shut in a box for a year with no natural light!

Evidently, he had been ill-treated because when someone came into the box, he shook like a leaf. However, he was lucky enough to have been bought by a man who loved him and took care of him.

The local people had come into contact with him and, at least, he stuck his head out of the window to watch. But it was impossible to put a bridle on him. Eventually, the person who ran the place managed to do it with a kind of fishing rod, in order to take him out and put him in a paddock. Nevertheless, it was very difficult to come into close contact with him because, when he was loose, he could not bear being touched, even though he wanted contact. He was terrified.

We decided to work with him during the course, because he really was a very interesting case. Even though my primary aim was to put a bridle on him, the first thing I had to do was to establish contact.

This is an essential point when we work with abused, ill-treated horses, who are very scared. Even if we have a goal, for example putting a bridle on him, it is necessary to observe the state in which the animal is, because if we do not pay attention to that, we can make mistakes and, if we do things quickly, we might make the situation worse. This is called "observing the steps": achieving every goal, no matter how small it is, until it is achieved, and only then passing on to the next goal, with patience and dedication.

When I entered the box, Negrito was shaking so badly that, in order to calm him down, I stood still, softly talking to him. I also used my body, openly, to bring him

Chapter IX

forward, since he kept moving backwards, and since I did not want to lose his contact, or expose myself to being kicked by him out of fear, I tried to make him smell the bridle, but he got really scared. So, I left him and then approached with my hand in a clenched fist, so that he would not think it was a claw.

His experiences with men had given him too many reasons to believe we were all dangerous. Little by little, I could touch him slightly, and I could even stroke him with the bridle on. When he relaxed and stopped trying to flee, I let him rest, as a reward for the huge step he had taken. We did this during the morning. Even though it may sound insignificant, it was a huge step for him.

Some people say that "brevity is the soul of wit" and this case was no exception. The horse needed to learn to trust, to start all over again. I truly felt that if I rushed, it could end up in disaster. Also, that morning, he had taken a homeopathic remedy called Arnica, extracted from Arnica montana, a plant known for its anti-inflammatory properties. Its ointment is used locally for bruises, traumas and even haemorrhages. Also, from a homeopathic perspective, it has a subtler use, when used in a higher potentiation – like the 200 grams he had – acting both at a physical and at a mental level. He was so traumatised, beaten and bruised, that Arnica 200 would probably help him overcome his fear of being beaten, which we proved later on.

When a horse has suffered so much, it is best not to put too much pressure on him, so that he can derive something positive to think and feel. In the afternoon, when we returned with the other assistants of the course, we had a surprise: an attendee was in his box giving him a massage on his neck and the horse was taking it well.

I came back to his box and his shuddering had diminished 50%. Since I wanted to work in a more open space so as to have more options of communication, we opened the box's door and let him out, while we all guided him into the paddock.

I left him in the paddock for some time so that he could investigate, walk, defaecate, urinate, smell and do everything he needed. Since we need the horse's attention to be able to work with him, it is best to first let him do what he needs until he is ready to pay attention. So I started examining him to see how to contact him, as shown in the first picture. When I came near him, he fled, so I made him flee a little more without too much pressure so that he saw me as a friend and not as a predator. Thus, little by little he fled less and tried to be nearer to me, but without allowing me to touch him. At times he needed to buck, which was useful because he really needed it. He had muscle contractions all over his body: spine, croup and hindquarters turned inside. I congratulated him with my voice every time he bucked because it was clear he did not do it to bother me, he simply did it out of a physical need of release. He had lost confidence in his own body.

This second step was also productive, since I could get closer to him and he started shaking less and less whenever I approached with my hand. I left him again when he showed more confidence. Next morning, when I got to the box, he was popping his little head out and willing to make more contact. He did not move back like the previous day. We all noticed this; besides, he looked much more relaxed, and when we took him out to the paddock his body was stretched and more open. His body and his eyes had recovered a lively expression. So I let myself be carried away by my intuition and, taking advantage of the fact that some children had come, I thought it would be good for him to be with them. The children cut a lot of green and fresh grass for him and one of them started feeding him. The horse took some bites and left. But every time he came closer.

We took the opportunity to observe this child's attitude, relaxed, trusting, friendly. Then, some little girls came over, who started feeding him from outside the paddock. So, when the situation was established, I suggested to them another working activity: to throw grass at his body. Since the animal was so afraid of contact, I thought that would be a soft way of desensitising him. So they started throwing him grass and making loud gestures and noises that could be taken as threatening. At first, he went back and watched. But every time he came back he started trusting a little more. From time to time I came into the paddock and made him work so that he accepted me. We bombarded him with apparently threatening but actually warm stimuli. In the end, he responded.

Here, at this stage, I'm adding a new stimulus; we started working with Eduardo to build the horse's trust.

Negrito starts trusting Eduardo and has enough courage to smell the halter he is so afraid of.

As can be seen in the picture above, one of the stimuli we used was the halter he was so terrified of. We changed a conditioned idea he had. We joined the halter with the grass and the calm voice as positive stimuli. He no longer fled as he had on the previous day, when, at the sight or smell of the halter, he started shaking and moving away.

Chapter IX

I started working again by putting pressure on him when he fled and staying still when he came closer; thus, the fleeing distance became shorter every time, by several inches. I did it with the bridle in my hand and without it. He finished the job relaxed, with a more open look and with an expression of surprise, as if saying: "I can communicate with some people without being hurt by them". This horse was very tame, he only needed to find a working environment suitable for his needs.

Here we can see Eduardo and the little girls sharing a moment with Negrito. We are desensitising him to people, grass, noises and the halter. Negrito came closer and closer to the children, who talked to him and threw him grass.

In the picture we can see how he mixed with all of us, eating, relaxed, with positive stimuli: contact with children, food, noises, the grass we threw him. All these actions aimed at making him feel at ease with humans.

My first work with him reached that stage, when we finished the course, but some of the assistants stayed in contact and were able to put the bridle on him. A few months later, he worked with other people, specialised in handling and natural taming. Therefore, everyone with their own technique, we all contributed to improving his situation. A few months later, I worked with him again, during another course, and he was 100 percent changed.

With care and patience, it is possible to change a negative situation for a positive one, when one is really intent on doing so.

WORKING TECHNIQUE

In order to work with horses with behavioural disorders, first it is necessary to have a clear picture of the situation, in order to make a diagnosis and a working plan.

First Step: Diagnosis

Horse's history: Gather all possible data that the people who are in charge of him can contribute: When did the horse arrive? In what state? How was the adaptation to the new place? What were his reactions, health and nutritional state? How was he handled?

Diagnosis: Stress due to stabling, fear of people. Terrible state of body tension.

Second step: Develop a prognosis

When we approach a horse that we do not know (especially if he has behavioural disorders), we do it carefully in order to observe his reactions: if he is calm, if he gets nervous or scared, if he is willing to have contact with people or if he moves away. We read his body, the signals, the signs, his skin's movements, his mouth, his eyes, how he looks at us, how he moves, his posture, if he is relaxed or excited, that is, we study all possible signs. In this case, it was obvious the horse wanted to have contact because he stuck his head out of the box, but when I approached him with my hand or came near him, he moved back, shaking. He had to defend himself since his memory was: humans equal danger.

The prognosis was as follows:

It is a case that requires a lot of patience; therefore, we should take careful steps, without rushing, in order to avoid making the situation worse. I did not know whether I would be able to put the bridle on him in those three days. The question that arose was: to what point will he accept me ? The point that he will accept will be the right thing for this horse at this moment.

In this situation, I worked with the following technique: I opened the box's door and calmly entered, in gentle and round movements, so as not to cause him more panic. With my body language, I indicated to him that he could trust me: when I approached him and he moved back, instead of shouting at him and putting more pressure on him, I also moved back, with my arm stretched to one side, not letting him move any further and, at the same time, I stared at him, paying attention to the

Chapter IX

moment when he stood still or moved forward and chewed. Then, I stopped staring at him as a reward, so as not to put so much pressure on him. If Negrito moved back to defend himself, I made him move forward. I showed him the direction towards which I wanted him to go. After doing this several times, he understood we could start "speaking" the same language. Thus, his fear began to diminish. Afterwards, I could put my hand closer to his neck to touch him without his moving back or shaking. As we started communicating, he began to chew, a sign of relaxation, which I encouraged with my voice and my body language.

Slowly, we started unblocking his language sequences.

How did he understand he was doing something right?

Through positive reinforcement. When he chewed and stopped shaking, I released the pressure and let him rest, "thinking", evaluating this situation with stimuli, responses and different proposals. Negrito expected to go through a traumatic situation again, because in his memory he had stored the information that a person inside a box with a bridle was something dangerous. However, this experience was different so he started evaluating the situation in another way. At this point, we began working with his mind, his memory; sending new, positive, stimulating signals, which the horse incorporated, evaluated and understood. His way of expressing this was to chew and stop shaking.

Third Step: Medication

As a veterinarian, I always aim at the animal's wellbeing. I prescribed, as I have said before, Arnica, which, like all well-prescribed homeopathic remedies, works in a mild, permanent and lasting manner. Arnica is advised when there is a bruised feeling, fear of contact and of being beaten and ill-treated. All these real symptoms Negrito showed, and rightfully so. The medication worked at a deep level, helping the animal overcome his traumas. Contrary to the usual belief (due to lack of accurate information), homeopathic remedies work quickly. The task of correcting behavioural disorders is optimised by using remedies that work on the animal's mood and mind, since they accelerate the process of physical and mental recovery because they act on the animal's vital energy, balancing what is unbalanced. In this case, it gave him back his trust and relaxed him so much that I was able to enter his corporal space quickly.

Horses have an oval corporal space around their body of approximately two meters. This space is as important for them as it is for humans. And they only open it when there is trust. If we watch a herd in a field, we will see that some horses ride together; for example, a mare with her foal, the stallion with the oldest mare or horses who were bred together.

Therefore, when a horse allows us to enter his space, it means that he trusts us. They build deep and intimate relationships that can last a lifetime, and miss their friends just as we miss ours. Even though Negrito needed contact, since his trust was broken, he reacted with his language: moving away, shaking and trying to avoid proximity. Honestly, it was not yet the right time to enter his corporal space.

Fourth Step: Change of circumstances

Work began in the afternoon. We observed him in a different environment: the paddock, because it is easier to observe a loose horse. He showed he had troubles moving, he was tense, due to lack of exercise and fear. The technique I used was to make him move. Since he went to the corners and did not let me come closer, I got him out of there so as to move him and not scare him too much. The fact that he wanted to buck, being such a repressed animal, was a healthy reaction. He did not do it to annoy me. Even as a technique, I encouraged him to buck again so that he could stretch his spine, which he did because he finished the work completely stretched, his hooves well on the ground and his eyes looked more natural and trusting. We always use what the animal gives us. Little by little, he started realising that he could move and use his body, and that he would not be punished for being a horse. So I decided to enter his body space a little further; I looked for him to have closer contact. If he fled when I approached him, I gently put some more pressure on him so as to make him run. Why? So that he understood I was his safety area. The result was that when he stayed close and allowed me to stroke him, I did not push him away. As he began understanding, he started letting me stroke him. When Negrito understood that being around me was safe, he stopped fleeing. Even though it was difficult for him, you could tell he really tried to understand what I asked him. My intention was to work as a reliable leader and he understood it that way. Little by little he let me stroke him and tried to be near me because he felt protected. When he chewed several times and stopped fleeing, I let him rest again as a reward. This is paramount; somehow, I had to tell him he was doing things right. It is a matter of quality and not quantity.

This is a highly effective technique because, when the horse understands what he is asked to do, and especially when he does it out of his own will, why should I continue insisting? it is more effective to leave him "thinking." They also assimilate their mental processes and, next time, we will take on where we left, instead of repeating the process all over again.

Chapter IX

Fifth step: Desensitisation

Next morning we took him to the paddock, where there were children whom he had worked with. Why? Because usually calm children have no expectations and act in a way that relaxes the animal. If our expectations are too high, we can miss what the horse can give us. The key is to pay attention to what he can actually do. I took advantage of this circumstance to carry out desensitisation work. How did we do it? We put a bale of grass in a corner of the paddock, the one chosen by him, where he felt more secure. When he went to eat, one of the children stood near holding the bridle. At first, it was difficult for him to stay but gradually he got used to it. Then, the boy moved the bridle abruptly and his reaction was to move away. But he started realising that the boy did not harm him. When some girls came, I used the same technique. They all threw him grass, all over his body. Of course, at first he got really scared. However, his reaction had nothing to do with fear, but with the memory of pain. This was the aim: to eliminate the memory of pain, the fear of pain. Many times, the horse's main problems were fear of pain, fear of punishment, fear of suffering. I wanted to prove to him that we did not intend to harm him, and he quickly understood, because he finally stayed eating near the children even though they kept throwing grass all over his body. These sudden, unexpected movements, from people he did not know, were a challenge for him which he could overcome very well.

Sixth (and last) step: Memory – Leaving him with the best memory

Since I only worked with him for two days, my goal was to leave him with a strong memory in his long-term memory. When he finished eating, I took him to another corner and stroked him with more strength, with a firmer intention in my hands, telling him "you can trust."

He let himself be stroked, he looked for me and stayed close, which proved the great advance he had made during the course. Therefore, at this stage I finished the work, knowing that he could always improve, as long as he was treated delicately and in his own language.

CONCLUSION

A few months later I worked with him again when I gave a course on massages. He was one of the horses with whom students practiced. He had contact with a lot of people with different degrees of sensitivity and tone in their body and hands. We were able to get inside his body space, massaging him on the abdomen, raising his hooves, his legs; we worked with him as if he had never had any problems. It is worth mentioning that this horse was a stallion and that there were also mares on the course. Even though he showed interest in them and got restless, he never stopped paying attention to the activities.

It was a great satisfaction to see his positive behavioural change, and to have a relationship with him as if he was a horse with no problems.

It is necessary to know the horse's language, in order to make an accurate diagnosis of his mental state, of what he can bear so as to modify his negative memories. The technique should be accompanied by sensitivity. Because if there is no sensitivity in understanding what the horse can bear, his condition can become much worse.

> *The key factors are:* **technique, perception, patience, flexibility and respect for the animal**

CHAPTER X

CASE III
PURITA

Horse in a Landscape (Marc – 1910)

A MARE FROM WHOM I LEARNT A LOT

A few years ago, a breeder of Spanish Anglo-Arab horses called me to see if I could do anything for Purita, a Spanish Anglo-Arab mare, who was 3 years old at that time. One day, she woke up lying on the floor, not being able to stand up, with a diagnosis of a fracture at the femur distal area near the femoral-tibial-patellar articulation. They did not know what had happened, only that the mare could not stand up; apparently, she had got stuck in the box, which was small. She was seen by three colleagues, who analysed her and suggested euthanasia. However, her owner and the man who ran the place felt they could do something for her, and every day they helped her to stand up, eat and recover. They did this for 6 months, until her owner called me to have a second opinion. During that visit, the little mare was pretty bad, her vertebral column was tense and inverted, she walked on three legs, as if jumping, the fractured left hind limb hardly touching the floor and crossed over the right one. But, she was full of life! Her owner loved her because she was his first filly, whom he was taming and who had proved to be very capable.

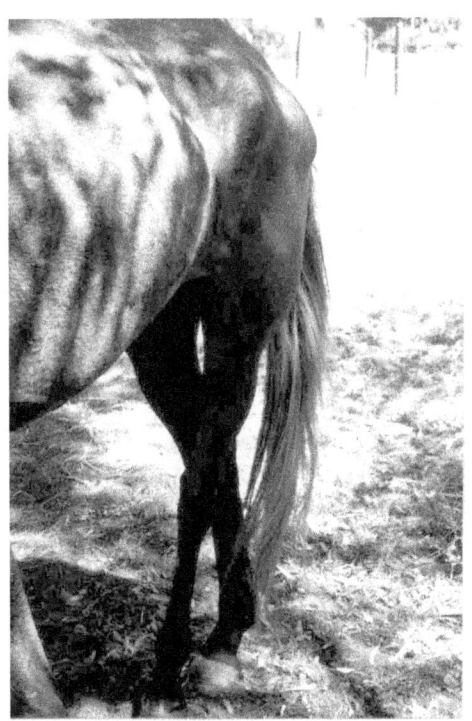

You can see the posture and condition of the fractured left hind limb, crossed over the right one.

Chapter X

Her owner was not convinced that the only solution was euthanasia. He was a religious man and did not feel he was the owner of the mare's life or death and because of this faith he kept on looking for another alternative.

After examining her and giving her a massage with the intention of making her relax and getting to know her better, I proposed to the owner an intensive treatment, aimed at making her feel as good as possible. Of course, I told him her recovery would take some time and that she would never be mounted again. But I was confident she could have a 60 percent recovery.

TREATMENT AIMS

- To recover the corporal conscience – body-mind integration.
- To recover the corporal conscience of the affected area.
- To work on the areas that had compensated in response to the pain.
- To widen the movement radius of the left hind limb.
- To rehabilitate the proprioception.
- To rebalance her.

In order to achieve these goals, I started the treatment with massages all over her body, so as to relax her. Through sensitive stimuli in different parts of her body, a motor response of relaxation was produced, due to the release of endorphins. When the mare relaxed, she could feel her entire body again, without so much fear or tension. She was in such a deep pain that some areas were sort of numb. I used balls to work on both sides of her spine, with a technique used in humans in cases of considerable tension. In this way, gently, she started relaxing her spine and, when she did so, she stretched. This is a communication and contact work, by means of which we show the animal he can do more than he believes. I taught the manager some of these simple massages, so that he gave her some for 5 or 10 minutes every day.

During the first month, I worked with her once a week. In every session, first I gave her massages all over her body and, each time, I focused on one thing.

One of the massages was aimed at the second objective, that is, working on the fractured limb. The croup's muscles were atrophied due to inactivity. In order to invigorate this area, that is, to make her aware of its existence, I also started with a different kind of soft massages. Mainly, I produced heat with my hands, with warm cloths soaked in essential oils with soothing anti-inflammatory properties and with friction and, at the same time, I ran my fingers over every muscle. At first, she seemed not to feel the area but, after the third session, she started showing more feeling, and even at times she tried to kick in order to defend herself. It was logical, because as we were working with more strength, she felt pain and wanted to protect herself. But also because she was very vulnerable and felt defenseless. You have to bear in mind that this mare would have been a prey in wild life. Therefore, I took this reaction as positive. She was "waking up", recovering her awareness.

At the same time, when she allowed me to work more deeply with her body, I started with another aim: treating the areas which had compensated for the pain. She had responded to the pain by twisting her spine and leaning strongly against the opposite side. Therefore, I needed to unblock the articulations of the back of the neck as much as possible in order to rebalance her, unblock the shoulder girdle in order to improve the front limb base of support, and keep on unblocking her spine.

Here you can see her body's tension and contraction and the atrophy due to inactivity of the croup's muscles

Since the manager massaged her spine every day, I worked with it by putting pressure on certain points in order to continue relaxing and stretching it. This work was permanent.

Together with body therapies, I prescribed different homeopathic remedies and Bach flowers. Homeopathic remedies reduce pain, tension and fear, while flowers help reduce stress due to illness. In fact, a month after we began the treatment, she showed

Chapter X

a 30 percent recovery: she was more relaxed, stretched, happy and walked a little better. And as she began to feel better, I could be more demanding. Furthermore the sesamoids of the suspensory tendon – the cord – of the right hoof were very swollen, because she hit it every time she stood up. This inflammation had been reduced 50 percent.

At that time, I decided to give her profound massages in the fractured limb. As the medial muscles of the leg were toneless, I began to rub them with essential oils and different levels of pressure to wake them up. From that moment on, she began to broaden the base of support, because when she became aware of the fact that the musculature was alive, she began to use it and move her best leg. Therefore, I continued the treatment with rehabilitation exercises. I made her walk from one side to the other, stimulating her to flex. It took her a lot of hard work, because she was accustomed to walking in a straight line so as not to feel pain. At the beginning, she walked slowly from one side to the other, but as we did this, she trusted a little more in her body and gained confidence.

At the same time, I worked with behavioural therapy. Why? Because Purita had lost certain social conditions due to the fact she was quite spoiled. She invaded our personal space, she wanted to walk in front of me, at times she got angry and tried to bite, or she wanted to play, depending on the day. It had been a long time since she last played! She was a rebel without malice. I simply reminded her of the social coexistence rules: respect for personal space – I prevented her from jumping at me; when she wanted to bite me, I anticipated her action with my voice; if she wanted to go ahead, I prevented her from doing so with my hand over her chest.

Step by step, she remembered the equine socialisation, and what was even more stimulating was that she gave more of herself to work happier. It was as if she had realised that she could move better than she "thought." When we arrived at this stage, I began with more demanding rehabilitation exercises. The manager of the place, an excellent collaborator, prepared a track with curves at one side and the other. He made her walk intently along the track. Essentially, he proposed movements that she did not do in her daily life, little challenges. This work was a physical, mental stimulus. Once she achieved that goal, we placed sticks on the ground, so she could learn to pass without touching them. This was a rehabilitation work on proprioception. At first, she touched them a few times, until she realised how she had to move her limbs. This exercise also worked well. I then decided to ask a little more of her. I began lunging her as if she were healthy. I always treated her as if she were healthy. That is to say, I worked mainly with her mind, because she was healthy and she had only one physical difficulty, an important but not fatal one. When I lunged her, one day, she wanted to buck on the left side. I remember the joy I felt that day. I told the manager: "Today, Purita is going to gallop." And so she did, when I let her loose, she stopped bucking, and began galloping and neighing with joy. She realised she could make a lot of movements she had stopped making. We continued with the treatment, spacing out the sessions I worked the joints of all the limbs, with movements of extension, flexion and rotation. Finally, I put a rope around the fractured leg and at the same time the manager made her walk in circles and I accompanied her trying to move her leg to the outside. After a few months, and after that exercise, it was possible to reposition that dislocated hip a little.

Now she lives with her sisters, she trots, gallops and bucks even if she is a little lame. Her spine is stretched, she recovered the atrophied musculature, she put on weight and she has a friend with whom she goes from one place to another.

I have learned a lot from her because she stimulated me to study, to look for rehabilitation exercises, to investigate and experiment. And she does not forget because every time she sees me, she comes to greet me. Every now and then I come to work with her and she loves it. The new manager at the farmhouse makes her do her stretching exercises and she accepts them just fine. We can trim her hooves – fix her hooves – because she learned to stand up. She got used to using her body intelligently. Unfortunately, euthanasia is practiced many times with animals that are actually recoverable. Many horses with bruises or traumas, apparently too impaired to compete again, are lost; animals that might be rehabilitated, just like many human beings are rehabilitated in an amazing way. I believe that we should be more careful before suggesting euthanasia.

My wish is that readers keep an open mind and learn to question.

There is still so much to learn about animals and with them. Finally, I dedicate this story from eastern tradition to my horse friends and my dear readers.

*Puríta with Gilberto, a laborer that helped her very much.
Note the left leg crossed over the right one in this picture.*

Chapter X

The man, the snake and the stone

One day a man who had not a care in the world was walking along a road. An unusual object to one side of him caught his eye. "I must find out what this is," he said to himself.

As he came up to it, he saw that it was a large, very flat stone.

"I must find out what is underneath this," he told himself. And he lifted the stone.

No sooner had he done so than he heard a loud, hissing sound, and a huge snake came gliding out from a hole under the stone. The man dropped the stone in alarm. The snake wound itself into a coil, and said to him:

"Now I am going to kill you, for I am a venomous snake."

"But I have released you," said the man, "how can you repay good with evil? Such an action would not constitute reasonable behaviour."

"In the first place," said the snake, "you lifted the stone from curiosity and in ignorance of the possible consequences. How can this now suddenly become 'I have released you'?"

"We must always try to return to reasonable behaviour, when we stop to think" murmured the man.

"Return to it when you think invoking it might suit your interests," said the snake.

"Yes," said the man, "I was a fool to expect reasonable behaviour from a snake."

"From a snake, expect snake-behaviour," said the snake. "To a snake, snake-behaviour is what can be regarded as reasonable."

"Now I am going to kill you," it continued.

"Please do not kill me," said the man, "give me another chance. You have taught me about curiosity, reasonable behaviour and snake-behaviour. Now you would kill me before I can put this knowledge into action."

"Very well," said the snake, "I shall give you another chance. I shall come along with you on your journey. We will ask the next creature whom we meet who shall be neither a man nor a snake, to judge between us."

The man agreed, and they started on their way.

Before long they came to a flock of sheep in a field. The snake stopped, and the man cried to the sheep;

Case III

"Sheep, sheep, please save me! This snake intends to kill me. If you tell him not to do so he will spare me. Give a verdict in my favour, for I am a man, the friend of sheep."

One of the sheep answered; "We have been put out into this field after serving a man for many years. We have given him wool year after year, and now that we are old, tomorrow he will kill us for mutton. That is the measure of the generosity of men. Snake, kill that man!"

The snake reared up and his green eyes glittered as he said to the man; "This is how your friends see you. I shudder to think what your enemies are like!"

"Give me one more chance," cried the man in desperation. "Please let us find someone else to give an opinion, so that my life may be spared."

"I do not want to be as unreasonable as you think I am," said the snake, "and I will therefore continue in accordance with your pattern, and not with mine. Let us ask the next individual whom we may meet - being neither a man nor a snake - what your fate is to be."

The man thanked the snake and they continued on their journey.

Presently they came upon a lone horse, standing tied up in a field. The snake addressed him; "Horse, horse, why are you tied up like that?"

The horse said; "For many years I served a man. He gave me food, which I had not asked for, and he taught me to serve him. He said that this was in exchange for the food and stable. Now that I am too infirm to work, he has decided to sell me soon for horsemeat. I am tied because the man thinks that if I roam over this field I will eat too much of his grass."

"Do not make this horse my judge, for God's sake!" exclaimed the man.

"According to our compact," said the snake inexorably, "this man and I have agreed to have our case judged by you."

He outlined the matter, and the horse said; "Snake, it is beyond my capabilities and not in my nature to kill a man. But I feel that you, as a snake, have no alternative but to do so if a man is in your power."

"If you will give me just one more chance," begged the man, "I am sure that something will come to my aid. I have been unlucky on this journey so far, and have only come across creatures who have a grudge. Let us therefore choose some animal which has no such knowledge and hence no general animosity towards my kind."

Chapter X

"People do not know snakes," said the snake, "and yet they seem to have a general animosity towards them. But I am willing to give you just one more chance."

They continued on their journey. Soon they saw a fox, lying asleep under a bush beside the road. The man woke the fox gently, and said; "Fear nothing, brother fox. My case is such-and-such, and my future depends upon your decision. The snake will give me no further chance, so only your generosity or altruism can help me."

The fox thought for a moment, and then he said; "I am not sure that only generosity or altruism can operate here. But I will engage myself in this matter. In order to come to a decision I must rely upon something more than hearsay. We must demonstrate it as well. Come, let us return to the beginning of your journey, and examine the facts on the spot."

They returned to where the first encounter had taken place.

"Now we will reconstruct the situation," said the fox; "snake, be so good as to take your place once more, in your hole under that flat stone."

The man lifted the stone, and the snake coiled itself up in the hollow beneath it. The man let the stone fall. The snake was now trapped again, and the fox turning to the man, said; "We have returned to the beginning. The snake cannot get out unless you release him. He leaves our story at this point."

"Thank you, thank you," said the man, his eyes full of tears.

"Thanks are not enough, brother," said the fox; "In addition to generosity and altruism there is the matter of my payment."

"How can you enforce payment?" asked the man.

"Anyone who can solve the problem which I have just concluded," said the fox, "is well able to take care of such a detail as that. I again invite you to recompense me, from fear if not from any sense of justice. Shall we call it, in your words, being 'reasonable'?"

The man said; "Very well, come to my house and I will give you a chicken."

They went to the man's house. The man went into his chicken-coop, and came back in a moment with a bulging sack. The fox seized it and was about to open it when the man said; "Friend fox, do not open the sack here. I have human neighbours and they should not know that I am co-operating with a fox. They might kill you, as well as censuring me."

"That is a reasonable thought," said the fox; "what do you suggest I do?"

"Do you see that clump of trees yonder?" said the man, pointing.

"Yes," said the fox.

"Run with the sack into that cover, and you will be able to enjoy your meal unmolested."

The fox ran off.

As soon as he reached the trees a party of hunters, whom the man knew would be there, caught him. He leaves our story here.

And the man? His future is yet to come.

BIBLIOGRAPHY

Bally, Gustav. *El juego como expresión de libertad* – Fondo de Cultura Económica, México, D. F., 1973.

Budd, Jackie. *Reading The Horse´s Mind*, Ringpress Books Ltd and Jackie Budd, Gloucestershire, UK, 1996.

Campbell, Edgard. *Paper: Comunicación: Algunos aspectos insólitos,* Institute for Cultural Research, London, U.K, pages 12 and 13, 1971.

Denoix, Jean-Marie., & Pailloux, Jean-Pierre. *Physical Therapy and Massage for the Horse,* Manson Publishing Ltd, 2001.

Diccionario de la Real Academia Española.

Gilson, Etienne. *El Tomismo - Introducción a la Filosofía de Santo Tomás de Aquino,* - Ed. Universidad de Navarra S.A, 1978.

Griffin, Donald R. *El pensamiento de los animales,* Ed. Ariel S.A, Buenos Aires, 1986.

Hernandez, Jose. *The Gaucho Martin Fierro,* Adapted form the Spanish and rendered into English verse by Walter Owen with drawings by Alberto Guiraldes, Farrar & Rinehart Incorporated, Murray Hill New York, 1936.

Kiley-Worthington M. Dr., *Teaching the horse, Horse & Rider*, Ed. Alison Bridge, UK, 1999.

Lathoud. Materia *Médica Homeopática.* Ed. Albatros. Buenos Aires, 1982.

Menescal, Vitor. *Studia Homeopática,* Vol. 1, E. Grupo de Estudos Homeopáticos, Brazil, J.T. Kent, Brazil, 1993.

Merino, Julio. *Caballos: historia, mito y leyenda,* Ediciones Compañía Literaria, Madrid, Spain, 1996.

Miller, Robert DVM. *Imprint training of the new born foal,* Ed. Pat Close, Published by Western Horseman Inc., Colorado, United States, 1995.

Morris, Desmond. *Guía para comprender a los caballos,* Emecé Editores S.A, 1990.

Rashid Mark, *Newsletter, 06/99.* United States.

Rees, Lucy. *La mente del caballo,* Noticias, Ávila, J. Spain.

Roberts, Monty. *The man who listens to horses,* Random House, New York, United States, 1997.

Saint Thomas Aquinas, Graduate Institute of International Studies James Tyler Kent.

Sheldrake, Rupert. *La conexión animal,* interview with Rupert Sheldrake performed by Marc Bekoff. Source: Bark Magazine, U.K.

Skipper, Lesley. *Dentro de la mente del caballo,* Horse&Rider, Ed. Alison Bridge, U.K., 1999.

Xenophon, *The Art of Horsemanship,* Translated by M. H. Morgan Ph. D, J. A. Allen & Company Limited, Great Britain, 1962.

Sufi stories of oral tradition

Anonymous, *Sufismo en Occidente, Preparación del Buscador,* Ed. Dervish Internacional, Buenos Aires, page 110, Story "El Hombre, la serpiente y la piedra", Version Idries Shah, 1994.

Saadi de Shiraz, *Cuentos de los derviches persas,* Version by Arthur Scholey, Story "La Soga", page 153, Arca de Sabiduría Collection, Ed. EDAF, Printed in Spain, original title: The discontented dervishes, April 2003.

Shah, Idries. *Cuentos de los Derviches,* Ed. Paidós Orientalia, Barcelona, Spain, page 237, Story "El Idiota y el Camello que pastaba", 1994.

Shah, Idries. *Las Hazañas del Incomparable Mulá Nasrudín*, Ed. Paidos Ibérica S.A., Barcelona, Story "Nunca se sabe cuando podría ser útil", page 18, Story "El Tonto", page 28, 1997.

Web bibliography

Przewalski Horses - http://www.treemail.nl/takh/

The process of taming, http://www.aamefe.org.ar

McMicken Donald, Biologic Basis of Submission, http://www.horsemagazine.com

Http://www.bbcmundo.com

Http://www.caballomania.com

Http://www.equinevetnet.com/animalscience/behavior/papers/learning.html

Http://www.un.org/spanish/works/environment/animalplanet/
horse.html/caballos_mongoles

Http://contexto-educativo.com.ar/2001/1/gardner.htm
Howard Gardner – Multiple intelligences

Http://www.geocities.com/gentenatural/mayo/inteligencia.htm
Howard Gardner – Multiple intelligences

Http://www3.rincondelvago.com/apuntes/descarga.php?00008340
Learning – habituation

Http://www3.uji.es/~agrandio/ACEDE98gran.htm
Imitative learning

Rupert Sheldrake, *An Experimental Test of the Hypothesis of Formative Causation* - Biology Forum, 85, (3/4) 431-443 (1992) - Http:// www.rupertsheldrake.org

Http://huitoto.udea.edu.co/Psicologia/glosario.html
Latent learning

Http://biocity.iespana.es/biocity/Etologia/apren.htm
Insight learning

Lojo María Rosa, *Facundo y El moro,* Peña, David. Juan Facundo Quiroga, Buenos Aires, Hyspamérica, 1986.- poem http://www.losandes.com.ar/2001/0401/nota8494_1.htm

O´Donnel Pacho, *El Águila Guerrera,* Quinta Parte, 1. El Moro, http://www.odonnell-historia.com.ar/anecdotario/EL%20AGUILA%20GUERRERA%20parte%20V.htm

Spacial-learning
Http://www.psychology.soton.ac.uk/External/Research/ResearchGroups/LearningAndBehaviourAnalysis/Overview.htm

Sufi stories

http://mamun-godagari.blogspot.com/2009/06/idiot-and-browsing-camel.html
The Idiot and the Browsing Camel

http://www.rodneyohebsion.com/mulla-nasrudin.htm
Grammar

http://www.i-c-r.org.uk/publications/monographarchive/Monograph2.pdf
Communication

http://home.primus.ca/~remedy3/THE%20MAN%20and%20THE%20SNAKE.htm
The Man, the Snake and the Stone

http://stories-shortstories.blogspot.com/2008/03/very-short-story-kindness.html
A Rope with a Name

http://www.livius.org/aj-al/alexander/alexander_t31.html
Alexander and Bucephalous

www.ingramcontent.com/pod-product-compliance
Lightning Source LLC
Chambersburg PA
CBHW081330230426
43667CB00018B/2889